The Black Feminist Coup

Elizabeth Powers
General Editor

vol. 19

The Black Feminist Coup

Black Women's Lived Experiences in White Supremacist Feminist Academic Spaces

Jennifer L. Richardson, Mariam Konaté, Staci Perryman-Clark, Olivia Marie McLaughlin, and Keiondra Grace

PETER LANG
New York - Berlin - Bruxelles - Chennai - Lausanne - Oxford

Library of Congress Cataloging-in-Publication Data

Names: Richardson, Jennifer L.
Title: The Black feminist coup: Black women's lived experiences in White supremacist feminist academic spaces / Jennifer L. Richardson,
Mariam Konaté, Staci M. Perryman-Clark, Olivia Marie McLaughlin, Keiondra Grace.
Description: New York: Peter Lang, 2024. | Series: Equity in higher education theory, policy, and praxis, 2330-4502; Vol. 19 | Includes bibliographical references and index.
Identifiers: LCCN 2023051283 (print) | LCCN 2023051284 (ebook) | ISBN 9781636677064 (paperback) | ISBN 9781636677682 (hardback) | ISBN 9781636677699 (pdf) | ISBN 9781636677705 (epub)
Subjects: LCSH: African American women college teachers. | African American women in higher education. | African American feminists. | Feminism and education—United States. | Women's studies—United States. | African American women--Study and teaching (Higher) | Feminism—Study and teaching (Higher)—United States.
Classification: LCC LB2332.32. B529 2024 (print) | LCC LB2332.32 (ebook)
DDC 378.1/208996073—dc23/eng/20231204
LC record available at https://lccn.loc.gov/2023051283
LC ebook record available at https://lccn.loc.gov/2023051284
DOI 10.3726/b21464

Bibliographic information published by the Deutsche Nationalbibliothek.
The German National Library lists this publication in the German National Bibliography; detailed bibliographic data is available on the Internet at http://dnb.d-nb.de.

Cover design by Jonnea J. Herman

ISSN 2330-4502 (print)
ISSN 2330-4510 (online)
ISBN 9781636677682 (hardback)
ISBN 9781636677064 (paperback)
ISBN 9781636677699 (ebook pdf)
ISBN 9781636677705 (epub)
DOI 10.3726/b21464

© 2024 Peter Lang Group AG, Lausanne
Published by Peter Lang Publishing Inc., New York, USA
info@peterlang.com - www.peterlang.com

All rights reserved.
All parts of this publication are protected by copyright.
Any utilization outside the strict limits of the copyright law, without the permission of the publisher, is forbidden and liable to prosecution.
This applies in particular to reproductions, translations, microfilming, and storage and processing in electronic retrieval systems.

This publication has been peer reviewed.

CONTENTS

Preface vii

Chapter 1 Introduction
Comparing Notes: Black Women in Isolation 1

Chapter 2 Black Feminist Genealogies and the Art of Storytelling 13

Chapter 3 Mariam's Story
Not in My Name: Harm, Accountability, and
Transformative Justice in Gender and Women's Studies 33

Chapter 4 Jennifer's Story
White Feminist Terrorism: But I Come with Receipts 55

Chapter 5 Staci's Story
Racism, Gender and Administration: The Perils of Healing
in Higher Education's Public Eye 81

Chapter 6 Keiondra and Olivia's Perspectives: Outsiders Looking In 97

Chapter 7   Conclusion: Sisterhood, Action Steps and Accountability   117

Epilogue Olivia's "Academic Karens" Reading List   147

References   149
Index   161
Author Biographies   165

PREFACE

F—Words from a Black Feminist and Ally Lens

#Fugitives. #Freedom. #Futures. #Feminism. This book is the product of a communion of three Black faculty women (and our co-conspirator students-turned peers) who found each other in a predominantly white (and predominantly hostile) public university in the Midwest United States. We crafted this book to demonstrate the range of consequences Black women face when attempting to resist white supremacy in the academy. More specifically, we focus on the particular frequency and vitriol with which white—and supposedly feminist—faculty women target their Black women colleagues. Indeed, the reader will observe "Karens" and "Beckys" entangled like weeds in almost every story recounted in this book (see Black Meme's Matter: #LivingWhileBlack With Becky and Karen by Williams, 2020 and The 5 Types of 'Becky' by Michael Harriot, 2017). We write this book in our pursuit of freedom and a future that enables us to thrive as teachers and scholars.

Despite what many of our women's studies students believe—that all social injustice will eventually die out with the old white men who run congress—it was actually white women who directly contributed to some of the most painful and harmful moments recounted here. From our standpoint, white women were truly the eye of the storm. While violent winds and torrential rains spiraled out from their location and into our direction, they went about their work of co-opting intersectionality and preaching about "diversity and inclusion," with an air of tranquility and ease. The disingenuousness of their actions both disturbed and enraged us. It was only by gathering together and telling our stories that we began to understand the extent and severity of racism and sexism in our institution; our gathering together was also the beginning of seeing a path forward through sisterhood, radical self-care, and strategies toward freedom.

The stories we recount here are not uncommon, but they are unique. Black women have long documented their mistreatment by the academy and by white feminists[1] (Crenshaw, 1989; Smith, 1989); a common thread of erasure, abuse, silencing, and violence runs through these stories. We add our voices to this history but maintain the uniqueness of our experiences. In her classic piece, *Black Feminist Thought* Patricia Hill Collins argues Black women share a "collective wisdom" (1990, p. 28), a particular standpoint formed by the composite experience of gender and racial oppression. While acknowledging the similarities in Black women's experience, Hill Collins argues that the value of Black feminist theorizing lies in its ability to account for the collective standpoint while identifying differences in experience. That we assert both the commonality and specificity of our experiences with sexism and racism is, in and of itself, Black feminist theorizing.

Our book is unique in that our stories often overlap as much of what we endured, we endured together as three of the only Black women tenure track faculty in the entire College of Arts and Sciences at the time we began writing this book. Often, institutions attempt to isolate Black people from each other under the hope and false assumption that our isolation will prevent our organizing. We were not isolated, however. On many occasions, we stood as each other's witnesses and co-conspirators, and we provided each other with support and comfort. Consequently, our stories are layered. They demonstrate the complexities associated with institutionalized racism and gender inequity, which often manifest in various collegial and academic relationships.

As individuals who comprise a collective, we occupy very different locations, not only in the matrix of domination, but also in academia. For instance, we all hold doctoral degrees but specialize in a variety of fields, including rhetoric and writing, sociology, African American studies, and gender and women's studies. We all identify as women, whereas four of us are Black one is white. Yet, we each live by Black feminist ideology and praxis. At the time when most of the events described in this book occurred, we all worked at the same Midwest university and represented three different departments across two colleges. Three of us worked as professors (Jennifer, Mariam, Staci) and two of us as doctoral students who have since earned their degrees (Keiondra and Olivia). As of the writing of this preface, four of us are faculty (two full professors—one with administrative experience—and two assistant professors) and one has carried her expertise outside of the academy to work in the non-profit sector.

Recognizing both the differences and similarities within our collective, we explore themes of racism, sexism, and white supremacist feminism within our various academic relationships and spaces. We explore the co-opting of intersectionality by white feminists and the weaponizing of diversity, equity, and inclusion by academia. We also reveal how we escaped our toxic professional relationships and forged new beginnings. But, as all Black feminist thinkers do (Hill Collins, 1990), we move beyond providing a criticism of white (feminist) supremacy in academia. To model a path forward, we explore the meaning of ally-ship, resistance, and the potential for radical, transformative change in hopes of making academia a more inclusive, affirming, and empowering space for Black people and Black women.

As a collective, it is important to note that each of us have touched, discussed and collaboratively written this book. Themes of what it means to be a fugitive, free, and feminist inform how we envision the future of Black women's labor in the academy. More specifically, this book explores intersecting narratives of how Black women faculty fled a racist and micro-aggressive gender and women's studies department, following the start of the COVID-19 pandemic and the 2020 summer of racial unrest. We subsequently moved to an institute that houses African American and African studies. We served as the first tenure-track faculty. On the one hand, this was difficult because predominantly white faculty had requested the institute as their home, but the dean had told them that there would be no tenure-track faculty in the unit, yet she reluctantly accepted our requests to transfer. Viewed in this light, folks questioned why Black women were allowed to do something that white faculty could not do. On the other hand, this provided us the benefit of innovating new teaching and scholarly opportunities, and the freedom to do so under spaces that were not white-centric. Recently-minted PhDs (former students) also lend voices to future possibilities of allyship in feminist spaces. On the other hand, despite opportunities to innovate and recreate, themes of misogynoir (Bailey, 2021) (including its resistance toward Black women's advancement) reflect a brutal irony that GWS and other departments continue to expect Black women to advocate for all women's and students' interests while focusing less on our own abilities to thrive. Even with the move to a new department home, institutions bear responsibility in providing Black women with an environment to thrive and dream of new possibilities and opportunities to develop curricula and initiatives that center Black lived experiences.

Bridging Black feminism, Black studies, sociology, and higher education, this book further surveys themes of trauma, pain, survival, sisterhood, and healing to offer future possibilities for dismantling and challenging white supremacy and misogynoir in the academy. It is timely and compelling work that blends methodologies of Black feminist collaborative scholarship with the future of Black studies during an era when Critical Race Theory (CRT) and anti-racist pedagogy are under assault by state legislators. Our work provides readers with a space to exercise academic freedom to call out white supremacy, especially in relation to white feminists and Black misogynists. Our candid accounts place the academy on notice, so those complicit in protecting white supremacist spaces will f*** around and find out.

Notes

1 It is important to note that we use the terms white feminists or white feminism in a variety of ways in this book. At times, we use the words, white feminist to describe white women who claim mainstream, orthodox, or popular feminism period. At times we use these terms interchangeably. We alternate between the terms orthodox feminism, mainstream feminism, white feminism, white supremacist feminism and the women's movement. Also, we capitalize Black and not white here as others before us (see Merriam Webster, 2021; Appiah, 2020; Bauder, 2020).

· 1 ·

INTRODUCTION
COMPARING NOTES: BLACK WOMEN IN ISOLATION

"There lies serious danger of romanticizing and/or appropriating the vision of the less powerful while claiming to see from their positions" (Donna Haraway, 1988, p. 415).

Black women's experiences of harm and the ways we've been institutionally deemed worthless and discredited inside and outside of the academy are well-documented in the works of Black women, scholars, and activists. So, too, are our experiences navigating often hostile white feminist spaces (Crenshaw, 1989; hooks, 2000a, 2014; Smith, 1989). Because the academy is so effective at isolating Black women, oftentimes Black women suffer silently in academic spaces. We are kept apart because as a collective we are viewed as a threat. Isolated, as the only one, we are not often able to "compare notes," leaving us isolated in what Melissa Harris-Perry (2011) calls our "crooked rooms." In this book, however, we offer our personal experiences as part of the long history and tradition of confronting the erasure, marginalization, and the strategic isolation of Black women.

Historically, white supremacist practices demand the isolation of Black folks in the hopes of impeding systemic, radical transformation and make progress toward eradicating systemic inequities (Schwitzer et al., 1999; Nelson et al., 2021). As a group of three Black faculty women (the only three Black women that were tenure track in the entire college—Jennifer, Mariam, and Staci), with few, but important allies (e.g., former graduate mentees Olivia and Keiondra), white feminist colleagues, along with others in positions of power and authority, perceived us as an even greater threat. This is evidenced by their pointed and purposeful attacks. Of the multiple strategies deployed against us, one of the most harmful was co-opting and weaponizing diversity and inclusion rhetoric, making it difficult for others to appreciate how we were being harmed; hence the epigraph by Haraway (1988), underscoring the danger this presents. White feminists have historically co-opted the language and practices of Black liberationists (Guy-Sheftall, 1995), but the last straw was when some of these white feminist colleagues used the murder of Black people in the summer of 2020 to advance their own special interests and financial goals. This is described in depth in Chapters 3 and 4. Gathering together and sharing our stories, we push back against this kind of feminism. We detail this brand of feminism later on in this chapter. It was only through holding one another in community that we were able to survive these experiences and escape to new beginnings.

In this book, we are not simply providing a criticism of white supremacist spaces in academia; we are also offering solutions to creating more inclusive, affirming, and empowering spaces for Black people and Black women in academia. Moreover, we are modeling a path forward for allyship between white feminist scholars and their Black counterparts in academia. Our experiences that we write about overlapped while at the same institution. Our stories provide layers and complexities associated with institutionalized racism and sexism at various stages and locations within academia (as both peers/faculty colleagues [Mariam, Staci, and Jennifer] and former peers/graduate students [Olivia and Keiondra] and as both Black women and our white woman ally). We each have unique positions from which we've witnessed and experienced shared trauma. But we've also charted together, pathways toward healing—intellectually, professionally, and emotionally. In this chapter, we explore the racist legacy of white feminism, wave theory, and Black feminism, as that history is linked to our own experiences that we write about in this book.

Black Women and Storytelling

Indeed, our experiences as Black women in academic spaces, which, ostensibly, tend toward our exclusion, are not only valuable, but they are also valid. In addition, our experiences increase our credibility as scholars and researchers who occupy what Audre Lorde refers to as a position of "outsiders within" (Lorde, 1984, p. 117). In this book, we attempt to create a space and platform to share our personal experiences combatting racism, marginalization, discounting, and erasure in white feminist circles. We believe our personal stories, although seemingly unique, represent the untold stories of so many other women of color in academia.

Storytelling is very important. "Many stories matter," as Adichie argues. "Stories have been used to dispossess and to malign. But stories can also be used to empower, and to humanize. Stories can break the dignity of a people. But stories can also repair that broken dignity" (Adichie, 2009 TEDGlobal). By offering our experiences, we hope to repair our collective broken dignity and empower other Black women in academia to share their own experiences. We also must underscore the fact that our collective experiences in academia are not isolated. Rather, they are telling of a long tradition of systemic white supremacist ideologies that were created to render us invisible, dispensable, and disposable.

Where's the Lie: Feminist Genealogies

In this section, we move from the importance of storytelling, toward a discussion of feminist genealogies. Understanding feminism and its evolutions are critical to understanding both Black feminism and its relationship to the stories we tell. There is no certification board or licensing exam required in order to identify as a "feminist." You don't need to apply for a membership, petition some local chapter for approval, or pass a standardized test. If you identify as a feminist, you are a feminist. Sure, someone might try to tell you differently, but their input will not result in a forfeiture of identity. And this is how it should be. One would be hard-pressed to find a vocal majority who wish to see feminism institutionalized in this way. After all, it is not hard to imagine how this kind of system could be used to exclude people not deemed "feminist" enough or "woman" enough. We already exclude people from feminist spaces, if not from identifying as a feminist. For example, groups like the National American Women's Suffrage Association adopted a separate but equal policy, barring Black women from their suffrage campaigns during the late nineteenth and early twentieth centuries (Rosenthal et al.,1985). Moreover, Wellesley College, one of the nation's oldest women's-only colleges, only started accepting trans women as students in 2017 (Binkley, 2017). Thus, we do not need to imagine a world where feminism is used to exclude people because this is already the reality of much of feminism. Despite these concerted efforts to exclude, "feminism is for everybody" (hooks, 2000b).

Following the white feminist movements of the late 20th century, hooks' statement was radical. hooks' scholarship pushed back against the "man-hating," female-only version of feminism popularized by an exclusionary group of privileged white women and proposed a new vision of feminism. She envisions a feminism empowered by difference and the quest for justice. Importantly though, when hooks writes "feminism is for everybody," she does not mean to suggest that feminism should operate as a "free for all" movement where "anything goes." Her goal is to demonstrate how feminism, at its fullest potential, can improve everyone's life, irrespective of their gender, race, and class. Indeed, feminists should maintain standards, and in the absence of the hypothetical scenario above, where feminism is totally institutionalized, individual feminists must enforce these standards and hold one another accountable. Historically, this has not been an easy task. Suffice it to say, the division of this labor has been anything but equal.

Black women are among the many women who have borne this burden. Historically, white women claim credit as the originators of feminist movement in the United States, but Black women's feminist organizing and theorizing dates back to the arrival of the first enslaved Black women in America, taking many forms over hundreds of years (Guy-Sheftall, 1995). Whereas mainstream (or white) feminist theories can be categorized in many different ways (Marxist, socialist, liberal, radical, cultural, etc.), Black women's theorizing is usually essentialized to "Third Wave Feminism" or "21st Century Feminism" (see: Archer Mann & Patterson, 2016; Tong, 1989; Donovan, 2006). While white women's feminist history and theory occupy a large swath of the canon, in the more mainstream works, any mention of Black women's feminist activism and theorizing is limited to one section of a book as merely a footnote to the broader scholarship. This is because Black women's theorizing tends to be essentialized and treated as a monolithic body of knowledge when, in fact, it is quite diverse and nuanced (Cooper, 2017).

Because of the diversity of Black women's intellectual and political perspectives, it can be quite difficult to provide a singular definition for a perspective that encompasses centuries' worth of intellectual theorizing, activism, and praxis. Thus, in an effort to acknowledge the plurality of Black women's contributions, many scholars find it useful to refer to Black feminisms rather than Black feminism. While Black feminists' theorizing does cover a wide variety of ideas (and even mediums), there are commonalities among African

American feminist thinkers (Guy-Sheftall & Sanders, 1996). First, all Black feminists acknowledge the particular forms of oppression experienced by Black women, where racism, sexism, and, at times, classism intersect, along with heterosexism, ableism, and transphobia. Second, Black feminisms view the oppression of Black women as inherently different from, and thus not as comparable to, the oppression experienced by white women and Black men (Hull et al., 1982).

Historically, movements for gender equality and racial justice have attempted to subsume the problems Black women face under the banner of sexism or racism (White, 1986). For example, Black women activists in the 1960s and 1970s were expected to choose between their allegiance to race over gender (Roth, 2004; Wallace, 1979). Third, Black feminists treat all oppression as interconnected and feeding into other forms of oppression (Combahee River Collective, 1977; Guy-Sheftall, 1995; Davis, 1983). Contrary to the theories discussed in the preceding sections, Black feminists do not attempt to identify a single source of oppression. Doing so, many argue, would result in splitting apart their various identities (Wing, 1997).

Fourth, and finally Black feminism is liberatory in nature. It emerges from the lived experience of women of color (Collins, 1990) and places a special emphasis on praxis. While the basic premises of Black feminism are fairly straightforward, as we attempt to provide an outline of Black feminist theorizing and activism over time, it should not be assumed that Black feminism is a homogeneous ideology (Guy-Sheftall, 1995). Since the early days of feminist movement (when even the word "feminism" had not yet been used) Black women have had to act as the moral arbiters of the movement, constantly pushing back while pressing forward. This is not a role Black women signed up for. However, many Black women participated in both abolition and suffrage movements, noting that both were imperative for the advancement of Black people (Terborg-Penn, 1998).

These Black women organized their own clubs and leagues—as well as participated and organized rallies and conventions—to address their unique set of issues at the intersections of race and gender, and also because they were largely denied access to white women's clubs. A clear manifestation of Black women's involvement in the women's rights movement can be seen through Sojourner Truth. Truth's speech "Ain't I a Woman" at the 1850 Women's Right Convention, eloquently summarizes the sentiments of Black women, highlighting the links between gender and race in their lives. During her speech, Truth shattered the shared consensus of womanhood by including the experiences of poor Black women, thus calling out the surrounding white feminists for their racism and class bias (Pough, 2004). Truth said,

> That man over there says that women need to be helped into carriages, and lifted over ditches, and to have the best places everywhere. Nobody ever helps me into carriages, or over mud-puddles, or gives me any best place! And ain't I a woman? Look at me! (McKissick, 1992)

It is also important to note that white women co-opted Truth's image for their own purposes and tokenized Truth as a representation of Black feminism, while simultaneously excluding Black women from their movement (see Painter, 1996).

The ways in which racism has stifled the productivity of feminists is the most troubling consequence of white women's activism (theorizing, activity, praxis, behavior, etc.), second only to the pain and trauma they have inflicted on Black women. And despite claims of an intersectional acknowledgment that was supposed to be characteristic of this "third wave" of feminism, white womanhood remains centered in feminist activism and spaces. What we are trying to punctuate here is how damaging and vile the false alarm of third wave 'intersectional' feminism has and continues to be on the lives of Black women. For over 200 years, Black women's fight for justice required the exhaustive, and oftentimes dangerous work of splitting loyalties between Black men and white women without a commitment from allies to return the same loyalty.

The experiences we share, illustrate just how far we are from the "intersectional wave" proclaimed by white feminist academics in the late 1990s. Here we reveal how claims of an intersectional takeover have done little more than obscure the continued exploitation of Black women in the academy while their white colleagues act as both accessories and accomplices to their suffering. Indeed, what this book ultimately reveals is that identification with intersectionality does not make one an intersectional feminist. If anything, outwardly claiming intersectionality has only made it easier for Ivory Tower "Beckys" (see Michael Harriott's "The Five Types of Beckys," 2017), "Karens", and "Miss Anns" to role play antebellum feminism in 21st century garb.

Our institutional experiences with white women's appropriations of intersectionality and superficial claims by white feminists that they acknowledge intersectionality are no different. We document how white women have consistently prioritized their own upward mobility in a violent social hierarchy rather than conspire with Black women to abolish the hierarchy altogether.

We also highlight how, in the reality of institutional racism, white women do not build alliances with the understanding that the intersectional subject position of Black women provides critical challenges for how Black women navigate institutional and white supremacist spaces. Audre Lorde, in her book titled, *Sister Outsider: Essays and Speeches* (1984) states that there cannot be a real and inclusive discussion of feminist theory if we do not include the input and lived experiences of poor women, Black women, and lesbian women. She goes on to make the point that Black and lesbian women cannot not be called upon to educate white women. She argues that racism and homophobia are real conditions for many and should be dismantled. She also makes the argument that "the master's tool will never dismantle the master's house" (p. 112).

Advocating the mere tolerance of difference between women is the grossest type of reformism. It is the total denial of the creative function of difference in our lives. Difference must not be merely tolerated; difference must also acknowledge inequalities that exist from our experiences as contrasts to white mainstream experiences. Only then does the necessity for interdependency become nonthreatening. Only within that interdependency of different strengths—both acknowledged and equal—can the power to seek new epistemological frameworks, expand our courage and sustenance through new charters. Within the interdependence of mutual (nondominant) differences lies that security which enables us to descend into the chaos of knowledge and return with true visions of our future, along with the concomitant power to effect those changes which can bring that future into being. Difference is that raw and powerful connection from which our personal power is forged (Lorde, pp. 111–112).

Our goal for writing this book, then, is to highlight superficial claims of intersectionality, while also modeling a path forward for allyship. "Modeling a path forward for allyship" is tantamount to a concerted effort to end racism; bridge building. Put simply, bridge building is real allyship: It builds alliances between Black people's (including Black women's) rights and women's rights as opposed to ignoring Black women's rights altogether. In her book titled, *Ain't I A Woman: Black Women and Feminism* (1981), bell hooks explains the existence of racism within the women's rights movement and the purpose it serves for white women. On the issue of the accountability of white women, she states that they used racism "to advance their own cause at the expense of black people" (p. 127). hooks further adds:

> Just as 19th century white women's rights advocates attempted to make synonymous their lot with that of the Black slave was aimed at drawing attention away from the slave toward themselves, contemporary white feminists have used the same metaphor to attract attention to their concerns... No other group in America has used Black people as metaphors as extensively as white women involved in the women's movement. (p. 141)

As hooks emphasizes, no sisterhood was possible without the acknowledgment of the specific conditions of Black women in America. The sisterhood that is necessary for the making of feminist revolution can be achieved only when all women disengage themselves from the hostility, jealousy, and competition with one another that has kept us vulnerable, weak, and unable to envision new realities. That sisterhood cannot be forgotten by the mere saying of words. It is the outcome of continued growth and change. It is a goal to be reached, a process of becoming. The process begins with the individual woman's acceptance that from a Eurocentric perspective, white women are often socialized to be racist, classist, and sexist, in varying degrees, and that labeling ourselves feminists does not change the fact that we must consciously work to rid ourselves of the legacy of negative socialization (hooks, 1981, p. 157).

Further, this illuminates the myriad ways in which the academy harbors white women and their violence. This book also highlights the magnitude of harm that Black women then must heal from and demands accountability from those who cause harm. The work then required of Black academic women has forever been to outperform our white peers, in our teaching, scholarship, and service, while knives are in our backs, faces and sides; as we simultaneously find ways to also be well and whole. However, we refuse to be quiet and complicit in recycling the weapons of psychological violence and tactics of anti-Black white feminists.

The Broader Implications of Anti-Blackness on Harm and Healing in the Academy

"Assumptions about racial and gender inequality play a central role in the questions that researchers ask and the kinds of projects social scientists pursue" (McClelland et al., 2020 pp. 3–4). As a methodology, what you are about to read is both a story—and a thread of stories that are interconnected and woven together in ways that explore themes of pain, trauma, healing and a future potential of refuge for Black feminist academics. While the themes of harm are carefully crafted into an overall Black feminist methodology that relies on story and collaboration, we also examine collectively the cognitive dissonances associated with doing women's work and undoing Black women's work. We would be remiss if we did not prepare you for some of the reactions you may experience. As such, we provide readers with this trigger warning: While the impact of our experiences is just as important as the methodology of storytelling itself, we recognize a variety of visceral reactions including BIPOC women who have been triggered by similar experiences.

Other triggering experiences may point to the blatant stereotypes and unreasonable expectations put upon Black women faculty, even in 2022, as we write this project. In her "crooked room" thesis, professor of political science Dr. Melissa Harris-Perry (2011) theorizes how stereotypes projected onto Black women keep them perpetually disoriented. As often as the academy serves as the voice of reason, challenging popular knowledge that has no basis in fact or reality, the academy also serves as a mirror—reflecting images and ideas in popular culture. As we recognize how our stories can be difficult to digest, we want to also remind readers that we have come through our experiences evermore committed to the beliefs toward allyship and support of Black women that Mia McKenzie (2015) brings forth in "'How Can White Women Include Women of Color In Feminism?' Is A Bad Question. Here's Why."

Many scholars acknowledge that the academy often produces the same anti-Blackness and sexism about which academics publish. Academics are also quick to point out that sexism and anti-Blackness are not simply inflicted upon the Black women within the academy. To be sure, the violences of academia extends beyond the conference rooms, classrooms, and hallways of our institutions and into our research designs, grant proposals, and policy recommendations. Many of the paradigm shifts and social policies most detrimental to Black women were born out of racist-sexist research and scholarly theories that were embraced long enough to cause extreme harm.

A classic example of how racism and sexism in academia affirm violence against Black women beyond academia is the moral panic of the "crack babies," a derogatory phrase that points to the purported use of prenatal cocaine. Although the myth of the crack babies originated in the white mainstream press, academic researchers were quick to "jump on the crack babies bandwagon" (Ortiz & Briggs, 2003). Although contemporary research (Hurt et al., 1997) and later studies (Betancourt et al., 2011) were unable to support the idea that prenatal cocaine use resulted in negative effects on the child, between 1985 and 2000, over 200 Black women were criminally prosecuted on charges of trafficking drugs to a minor, child abuse, and manslaughter (Lester et al., 2004).

While some women were put behind bars, many, many more had their parental rights taken away and were forced to release their children into the foster care system. Because very few pregnant white women were tested for drugs, Black women were disproportionately represented in the rates of those prosecuted and penalized for prenatal drug use. Researchers aided and abetted this attack on Black mothers by favoring findings that demonstrated a profound, negative impact on maternal cocaine use. In reference to an annual meeting of the Society of Pediatric Research, Ortiz and Briggs (2003) explain: "Studies that showed no effect on a pregnancy had an 11 percent acceptance rate, while those that found undesirable effects on fetuses had a 57 percent acceptance rate, despite the fact that negative studies tended to be better designed, more likely to have a control group, and more likely to compare polydrug exposure with and without cocaine" (p. 45). Good scientists don't ignore research that challenges their worldview. It seems academics were quick to abandon the scientific method when it required them to challenge their hatred of Black women.

These studies have had a profound effect on how we understand the harmful effects of negative racial stereotypes and biases in relation to research and scholarship. For example, published in 1965, Senator Daniel Patrick Moynihan's commissioned "study" on Black family structures infamously resulted in the demonization of Black womanhood and Black mothers. Serving as advisor to President Lyndon B. Johnson for his "War on Poverty," Moynihan's report gained him notoriety in academic circles, resulting in a subsequent appointment as faculty at Harvard University. While the previous examples demonstrate more blatant racism, we provide additional examples that suggest a more nuanced subtlety when applied to the academy. With these more nuanced examples, our stories reveal strong and direct connections. Later in this book, we identify examples of accusations and criminality, as well as negative stereotypes about Black womanhood. While this chapter provides an overview of some historic and classic challenges with white feminism, as placed in relation to white supremacy, this book seeks to take lessons learned from the past to move toward future possibilities.

In Chapter 2, "Feminist Genealogies and the Art of Storytelling" we discuss the legacy and importance of Black women's historical and contemporary collective spaces and oral traditions. In honoring the rich works of Black feminist thinkers and movement builders, we then discuss in further detail historical and formative contributions to Black feminisms. Here we are especially interested in providing insights into mainstream feminist revisionist histories as well as our praxis-based framework for those who may be new to Black feminist works and history.

In Chapter 3, "Mariam's Story: Not in My Name: Harm, Accountability, and Transformative Justice in Gender and Women's Studies," she shares her story of her exodus from the Department of Gender and Women's Studies, beginning with her appointment as a faculty member in the former Department of Africana Studies. We begin with Mariam's story as it offers compelling themes that explore the relationships between freedom, feminism, and futures, particularly in relation to intersectionality between race and gender. By sharing, Mariam challenges institutions to enact systems of accountability and freedom, as both are central to Black women's healing.

We continue in Chapter 4 with "Jennifer's Story: White Feminist Terrorism: But I Come with Receipts," which adds layers and dimensions to the toxicity and trauma experienced in a Gender and Women's Studies department where Mariam was also a faculty member. Her story further offers an in-depth discussion of offices of institutional equity and white supremacist higher education structures, and impeded freedom in the pursuit of justice and healing. As a pre-tenure professor, Jennifer offers an auto-ethnography which demonstrates liberation through truth telling.

In Chapter 5, "Staci's Story: Racism, Gender and Administration: The Perils of Healing in Higher Education's Public Eye," she presents a specific narrative about the relationships between white supremacy and misogynoir in higher education leadership, as also connected to offices of institutional equity. She also provides concluding remarks about her exodus from the same Gender and Women's Studies department where Mariam and Jennifer were faculty due to a negative recommendation the department provided as the secondary unit of her appointment. Finally, she provides concrete lessons for what it means to heal publicly from institutional oppression and provides reflections on future leadership moving forward through an Afrofuturistic lens.

Collectively, Chapters 3 through 5 provide specific narratives on the implications of trauma and healing as they apply to how Black women navigate higher education spaces. While these stories are triggering and make critical contributions to the literature of feminism, these contributions are not void of the opportunity for feminist allies and leaders to take critical steps toward action and accountability, which is why we include Chapter 6: "Keiondra and Olivia's Perspectives: Outsiders Looking In." Here Olivia (a feminist ally and former doctoral student) and Keiondra (a Black feminist, former doctoral student, and recent PhD grantee, who has left higher education to work in the private sector), lend voice to our narratives to hold peer white feminists and institutions accountable. The duality of perspectives and insights into critical whiteness studies are case-point examples for how Black and white feminists can work collaboratively to dismantle systems of oppression while also lending their voices to the trauma faced by Black women in the academy.

In Chapter 7, "Conclusion: Sisterhood, Action Steps and Accountability," Olivia begins by addressing the concept of sisterhood. She compares sisterhood as it is understood by white feminists and Black feminists and considers how antiracist white women and women of color have forged sisterly bonds in the past. Here, we also collectively discuss the importance of our sisterhood and relationships with our coconspirator, Olivia, who had our backs and earned our trust (more on Olivia's story later in this book). While Olivia acknowledges that she cannot say definitively that it is impossible for white women to contribute to Black feminist standpoints, she explains why she feels she is not in the position to do so considering both how she identifies racially and her specific research interests. From there, we collectively provide an outline that enacts bridge building and accountability. Finally, Olivia provides a concrete reading list for feminist co-conspirators to read in order to be stronger allies or "riders" for Black women.

In sum, our hope is to provide readers with a space to use academic freedom to call out white supremacy, especially in relation to white feminists. We also call for administrators to take notice and responsibility when harm and trauma happen under their care.

· 2 ·

BLACK FEMINIST GENEALOGIES AND THE ART OF STORYTELLING

As authors, we situate our stories and ally work within the context of other Black feminist stories. Before sharing our stories, however, this chapter presents a genealogy of Black feminist work to establish a context for understanding Black women's stories. The art of storytelling, moreover, requires that we affirm and acknowledge the traditions of Black feminist theories and storytelling as shared by Black women collectives and ancestors. The history of Black feminism must be positioned in relationship to the white mainstream suffrage movement in the United States, especially given that both the Atlantic Slave Trade and women's right to vote were two issues whose time periods exist in closer proximity. In tracing this genealogy, we also make the case as to why white feminism is not compatible or comparable to Black feminism. Because of the diversity of Black women's intellectual and political perspectives, it is beyond the scope of this chapter to provide a comprehensive discussion of the entirety of Black feminist contributions. In an effort to avoid essentializing the plurality of the tradition of Black feminist thought, we focus solely on the work of Black feminist scholarship most pertinent to the goals of this book.

Oral Traditions and the Silencing of Black Women

As a methodology, storytelling is a critical method for conducting qualitative research, and is rooted in a variety of oral traditions, including African Diaspora oral traditions (Banks-Wallace, 2002). Specifically of African American storytelling, JoAnne Banks-Wallace (2002, p. 411) contends that stories are often used as a means of preserving cultural memories and histories. Through the process of "storying," "elements previously viewed as disconnected and independent [are put] into focus as parts of a unified collage" (p. 417). Like all research methods and methodologies, the process of storying does not come without its own set of specific rules or conventions. While traditional qualitative research methods suggest listening to stories as a key convention, for African American storying, listening is not a specifically taught rule or convention: "Instead, the memory structures used to recognize and store stories are developed as a result of repeated exposure to oral stories (Champion, Katz, Muldrow, & Dail, 1999; Sutton-Smith, 1986). Storytelling allows us to share stories and our thoughts about them with others" (p. 417).

Deeply rooted in the African American tradition, are additional elements of storytelling. In particular, the role of elders in African American communities is essential to understanding the art of storytelling. As Chanee D. Fabius (2016, p. 424) writes,

> The life stories of African American elders are influenced by unique historical and personal events and circumstances. These stories are shared through the development of one's narrative identity, which enables individuals to interpret and explain life events in order to both learn more about who they are and to share with other people (McAdams & Cox, 2010). Among African Americans, storytelling has been a method of intergenerational communication and connectivity for centuries, as well as a way in which younger generations can learn about cultural and family values, and methods of resilience specific to the African American experience.

From our own experiences, we recognize and honor the lived experiences of academic elders whose stories are not shared in this space, yet who too have shared common themes of discrimination, racism and oppression across generations of academic work. It is perhaps, however, one of the central reasons as to why we situate our work within Black feminist genealogies as they connect with storytelling.

While storytelling is rooted in many cultural oral traditions, including African American traditions, it offers points of intersectionality with both Black and feminist qualitative research methods. While African American storytelling is a key cultural practice, foundational to understanding Black oral traditions, in white feminist research, Black women's stories often become erased. As noted by Julia Jordan-Zachery (2013, p. 103), "As a concept, intersectionality has gained increased popularity among some feminists and other scholars. This is occurring at the same time that Black women seem to be disappearing from political science scholarly works, for example. Additionally, Black women are rarely treated as research subjects, particularly in intersectionality research." Jordan-Zachery, moreover, concludes her narrative analysis of Black feminism and storytelling in political science research by specifying the following:

> Stories can be used to maintain "existing structures of domination" (hooks, 1991), but they can also be used to emancipate (Clough, 2002) the oppressed and challenge multiple systems that result in marginalization. The use of Black women's narratives can be instrumental in responding to the silencing and omission of Black women in political science research in general and intersectional research more specifically, and they can expand our understanding of politics and how it is experienced and performed by multiple groups. (p. 117)

Though Jordan-Zachery's work is specifically applied to political science research, it is important to emphasize here that the erasure of Black women's experiences by white feminism crosses a multitude of academic disciplinary and even mainstream popular and trade publications. Before analyzing feminist publications like UK's *The Guardian* in their erasure of Black feminist experiences, Terese Jonsson (2014, p. 1014) reminds us of how she defines white feminism by the following:

> White feminism is not any feminism espoused by white feminists, but rather an articulation of feminist politics which is inattentive to histories of colonisation and racism, and thus "subsists through a failure to consider both the wider social and political context of power in which feminist utterances and actions take place, and the ability of feminism to influence that context. (Aziz 1992, p. 296)

Jonsson further identifies three patterns of problematization when analyzing three white feminist narratives in *The Guardian*: "These texts identify three (intersecting) patterns of problematic representations as connected to the erasure of Black feminist stories: (1) silencing and marginalisation; (2)

visibility in the form of inclusion politics; and (3) appropriation and misrepresentation" (p. 1017). In other words, Black feminist stories (as acknowledged in both mainstream and academic spaces) are silenced and marginalized compared to mainstream feminist stories, and when they are included, they are used for mere virtue signaling in a way that provides lip service to diversity and inclusion. Other times when Black women's stories are included, they are often misconstrued and misused by mainstream media and academic spaces to advance a narrative that aligns more closely with whiteness. Tema Okun's work (2021) further provides context for our understanding of the ways white supremacy culture operates. These problematic representations can be seen as we trace the genealogy of orthodox feminist history, prioritizing the story and legacy of Black women story-tellers and truth-telling from Black Feminisms.

Despite efforts to erase Black lived experiences, storytelling by elders—including and especially Black women–have tremendously helped to sustain Black oral traditions. For example, the horrendous circumstances of slavery dating back to 1619 inspired Black women's first yearnings for freedom and rebellion. Scholars have noted the multitude of ways in which enslaved Black women resisted the sexual assaults of white men, defended their families, and participated in revolts (Davis, 1971). Early Black feminist resistance to specifically gendered oppression can be seen through the refusal to bare children into slavery using forced natural abortion and birth control methods and fighting back against rape. These techniques can be considered evidence of a Black feminist consciousness because they demonstrate an awareness of oppression, both as Black people and as women. Stories such as these are conveniently left out of first wave analogies, because they predate—but also happened during—the abolition movement, and compromise the conventional mainstream narrative that United States feminism began with white women.

The first wave of mainstream feminism is often associated with liberal feminism. American liberal feminism is popularly regarded as the school of thought that began with the Seneca Falls Convention in 1848, which subsequently birthed the movement for women's suffrage (Jaggar, 1983; Tong, 1989). More accurately however, liberal feminism was just one school of thought that contributed to the formation of what is known as the "first wave" of mainstream feminism, whose leaders included Lucy Stone, Elizabeth Cady Stanton, and Susan B. Anthony. Liberal feminism is named as such because it adopted its ideals from enlightenment liberalism popular in 17th- and 18th-century Western Europe. Enlightenment values posited that individuals have inalienable or "natural" rights that should not be taken away. Liberal feminists believe that both women and men should be unobstructed in their pursuit of self-fulfillment, autonomy, and equality. Of specific importance to early liberal feminists was the right to vote, own property, and receive an education comparable to that of men's (Donovan, 1996). Women of the early 19th century wanted to be seen as individuals, not as extensions of their male partners or parents and believed that these could be achieved by working within the existing social structure. As such, liberal feminists maintain that should women be allowed to develop their own reason through education, they will be able to reject traditional gender roles and compete in society as equal to men (Tong, 1989).

Both Elizabeth Cady Stanton and Susan B. Anthony, beloved among white feminist for their contribution to not only liberal feminism but white women's suffrage, supported politicians who favored white supremacy and "woman first, negro last" policies (Davis, 1991). In 1893, Susan B. Anthony, president of the National American Woman Suffrage Association, passed a resolution that "definitively accepted the fatal embrace of white supremacy" (Davis, 1991, p. 115) in the women's movement. This resolution implied that since "American" (i.e., bourgeoisie) women made up a greater percentage of literate voters, their rights were more important than the rights of Black women, immigrant women, and their male counterparts. In the same year, the Supreme Court reversed the Civil Rights Act of 1875, granting judicial sanction to Jim Crow and lynch law (Davis, 1991).

Early Black Feminism

During what is considered the first wave of feminism, a majority of Black women were enslaved (Taylor, 1998), but there were also free northern Black women—typically abolitionists—that could not escape the harmful myths about Black womanhood which blamed them for their victimization. Therefore, these women organized against racial and sexual oppression simultaneously. While they advocated for the interconnectedness of their oppression on the grounds of their sex and race, they too are often left outside of narratives about gender activism, due to the entanglement of their race efforts. The model for feminist activism in the mainstream has become plagued by the idea that a real feminist movement must be one that makes claims solely on the basis of gender, which contributes to the exclusion of Black women's feminist efforts (Roth, 2004). The notion of the feminist movement being solely based around gender is precisely what divided Black and white abolitionists, especially as it pertained to the 15th Amendment. However, many Black women participated in both abolition and suffrage movements, noting that both were imperative for the advancement of Black people.

Abolitionist frameworks as well as early Black feminist thought greatly contributed to suffrage (Davis, 1991). Beverly Guy-Sheftall's *Words of Fire: An Anthology of African American Feminist Thought* (1995) is perhaps one of the most comprehensive efforts to chronicle the non-fiction works by Black feminists. In this anthology, the whitewashing of feminism is laid bare. Contrary to the orthodox retelling of United States feminist history which tends to point to the start of the "third wave" (i.e., the early 1990s) as the inception point of Black feminisms, *Words of Fire* documents Black women's participation in public discourse on women's rights as early as the 19th century. Even among these early Black feminists we see evidence of an intersectional consciousness. Whereas white feminist activism was almost entirely limited to the struggle for suffrage, Black women spoke on behalf of many intersecting issues. They organized their own clubs and leagues—as well as participated and organized rallies and conventions—to address their unique set of issues, such as Black womanhood, uplifting the Black community, and improving family life, and also because they were largely denied access to white women's clubs. For example, the Salem Massachusetts Female Anti-Slavery Society was founded in 1832, a year before the nationally recognized all-male American Anti-Slavery Society (AAS), or the convergence of white female abolition efforts.

While white women suffragists wanted to focus the movement as more closely aligned with feminism, perhaps one could argue that the "mainstream" white feminist, or women's movement, developed in relation to the abolition movement. As it is well documented, white women learned how to be activists by observing Black abolitionists (Yee, 1992; Davis, 1983). Beginning in the 1830s, poor and wealthy white women alike aligned with the abolitionist movement, seeing a connection between their own plight and the oppression of enslaved peoples. Despite the sexism they encountered in organizations like the American Anti-Slavery Society, white women played an important role. Poor white women donated what little money they made from working in mills and textile factories to anti-slavery campaigns while wealthy white women donated their time. The extent of white women's involvement in abolitionist movements is documented in detail by Angela Davis in *Women, Race and Class* (1983). She writes, "Women developed fund-raising skills, they learned how to distribute literature, how to call meetings—and some of them even became efficient public speakers. Most important of all, they became efficient in the use of the petition, which would become the central tactical weapon of the women's rights campaign" (p. 39).

In addition to gaining practical knowledge on how to organize, white women also learned about the nature of oppression. Their exposure to sexism in anti-slavery societies taught them how to resist misogyny both in the political arena and in their personal lives. This is how the suffrage movement was born—out of a recognition that if women were to make a meaningful difference in the abolition movement, they must force society to allow their participation in civil society. After the passage of the thirteenth amendment, the tensions between feminists and abolitionists came to a head over the issue of Black male suffrage. Davis (1983) contends that these tensions existed primarily because, although white feminists abhorred slavery on moral grounds, they failed to recognize or promote the anti-racist consciousness that would have enabled them to realize the urgency of Black peoples' situation compared to their own. When push came to shove, white women were not willing to center the needs of Black people if it meant momentarily deprioritizing their goal of obtaining their own suffrage. Thus, in relatively short order, white women resorted to white supremacy. In an 1865 letter to the editor of the New York Standard, Elizabeth Cady Stanton—prominent white suffragist—stated:

> This is the negro's hour. Are we sure that he, once entrenched in all his inalienable rights, may not be an added power to hold us at bay? Have not "black male citizens" been heard to say they doubted the wisdom of extending the right of suffrage to women? Why should the African prove more just and generous than his Saxon compeers? If the two million Southern Black women are not to be secured the rights of person, property, wages and children, their emancipation is but another form of slavery. In fact, it is better to be the slave of an educated white man, than of a degraded black one… (Davis, 1983, p. 70)

Clearly, Stanton did not wish to advance Black progress if it meant white women were not able to immediately reap the benefits of that progress. Moreover, we learn from this passage that, despite deploying "the metaphor of slavery" often as a way to describe white women's sexual oppression, Stanton failed to recognize the political and historical relationship between the oppression of white women and that of Black people. Such a recognition would not have been novel at the time. However, Stanton's advocacy for Black women is superficial in that our mention is nothing more than an effort to gain enfranchisement for white women. Her manipulation of Black womanhood can be seen as a source of the less than sisterly legacy between Black and white women that outlasted the passage of the 19th Amendment, which failed to address Black women's and men's disenfranchisement in the south, and continues to exist today. White women gained their oration, organizing, writing, and agitation skills from their work in the abolitionist movements, often alongside and with input from Black women and men, including Frederick Douglas. Yet, the articulation of their opposition to the suffrage of Black men invoked the privileges of white supremacy and highlighted the superficial nature of their campaigns for Black equality.

The passage of the fifteenth amendment lit the fire for a distinct white women's suffrage movement. Black women were prolific in the suffrage movement despite resistance from white women who wanted the vote exclusively for themselves (Giddings, 1984). Black women organized many voter leagues and clubs, such as Mary Shadd Cary's Colored Women's Progressive Franchise Association in Washington D.C. whose primary goal was suffrage for Black women. Further, the first convention of Black women's clubs took place in Boston in 1895 with the agenda of Black female empowerment for the individual and the advancement of the race (Guy-Sheftall, 1995). Through that convention a number of Black women's clubs condensed into the National Association for Colored Women (NACW), a federation that sought to promote self-help and racial uplift. Under the leadership of Mary Church Terrell, the NACW also supported women's suffrage.

Mid-20th Century Black Feminism: Black Liberation and the Second Wave

Black feminist activism during the second wave is similar to the activism of the first wave. Primarily, the second wave of mainstream feminism is often associated with radical feminism. Radical feminism developed in the late 1960s and is actually just an umbrella term that encompasses a wide variety of feminist thought existing under the assumption that gender systems should be condemned and eliminated, sexism is the foremost form of oppression, and biology plays a key role in the oppression of women (Tong, 1989). Black feminism occurring during what is typically discussed as the second wave, continues to address the exclusion of Black women's issues in primary social movements of the time. Black women sought to negotiate their roles in two perceptually distinct movements—Black liberation struggles and the women's liberation movement of the 1960s and 1970s (Taylor, 1998). Both the Black liberation struggles and the second wave feminist movement took up single-issue perspectives that largely left the issues of Black women unaddressed. However, Black women continued to develop their distinct feminism based on the recognition of the complex interplay of race, class and gender in their lived experiences.

The Civil Rights movement of the 1950s and 1960s featured Black women activists in a variety of roles. In the foremost years of the Black rights struggle, Black women worked alongside Black men who valued the input and networks of southern Black women (Roth, 2004). The work of Black women can particularly be seen in the student coordinated non-violence efforts. Students of the time, initiated sit-ins and freedom rides to expose the racial violence of whites during the time, and about 48% of those student participants were Black women (Roth, 2004). Furthermore, it is noted that the organizations of the time were political training grounds for feminism for both Black and white women (Giddings, 1984; Taylor, 1998).

While the numbers of women present in the struggles for civil rights were numerous and many of the women expressed "shared unity of purpose and camaraderie" (Giddings, 1984, p. 311) within the movement, male chauvinism was nonetheless present, and feminist dissent began to fester. Women that played prominent roles in the movement also spoke out and were critical of the male figures. One notable figure is Ella Baker, a former field secretary of the NAACP, director of the Southern Christian Leadership Conference (SCLC), and organizer of the Student Nonviolent Coordinating Committee (SNCC). Baker often stated that she enjoyed the backstage position she played in the movement but also expressed that she did not believe she had a place in the movement being a woman and also not a minister. That said, she was a critic of Dr. Martin Luther King, Jr. whose leadership emphasized a pulpit to pew model, while Baker's "entailed cultivating potential in others" (DeLaure, 2008). She expressed that leaders in the organizations viewed the role of women organizers as similar to those of women in the church, "taking orders and not providing leadership" (Giddings, 1984). There were also accounts of Dr. King being uncomfortable with women who spoke out, and taking the ideas of women's organizations without credence (Giddings, 1984). When speaking specifically of the tensions between Baker and King, "Baker grew increasingly frustrated that many of the SCLC ministers were unwilling to get involved in voter registration in their hometowns..." and that the SCLC "seemed more interested in establishing King as a national icon, a Moses-like savior who would free his people from modern-day slavery, than in working on grassroots organizing" (Olson, 2001, p. 144).

Following the Civil Rights Act of 1964 and Voting Rights Act of 1965, as well as the murder of Dr. King, Malcolm X, and other prominent figures in the movement, the tide of the struggle shifted to a Black nationalist trend (Roth, 2004). This shift is noted as profound for the development of Black feminist collective consciousness in the second wave (Giddings, 1984; Guy-Sheftall, 1995; Roth, 2004; Taylor, 1998). The emergence of Black Power rhetoric reinforced a masculinized discourse and practices that led to the silencing and minimizing of Black women's roles in the movement. According to the nationalist sentiments of the Black power movement and subsequently the Black Panther party, as noted by Giddings, the truly "revolutionary" role of Black women was a supportive one in which they kept the house while the Black man kept revolution and reclaimed his public manhood (Giddings, 1984). The masculinity demonstrated in Black nationalist rhetoric has been explained by Black feminist scholars as a response to the Black matriarchy theory put forth in the 1965 Moynihan report (Davis, 1971; Giddings, 1984; Roth, 2004). The attack on the Black family put forth through the state with that report, had a devastating effect on the relationship of Black men and women, with a lot of Black feminist literature responding to the aftereffects of the report.

For example, noted Black feminist scholar Angela Davis served as a public presence within the Black nationalist organizing of the late 1960s. However, she noted the ill relationship of men and women in militant organizations caused her to leave the movement:

> I was criticized very heavily, especially by male members of [Ron] Karenga's [US] organization, for doing a "man's job." Women should not play leadership roles, they insisted. A woman was to "inspire" her man and educate his children (Giddings, 1984, p. 316).

The quote delivered by Davis at an organizing event in San Diego highlights the tenuous relationship for Black women in the struggles for Black liberation. The roles they served in the early civil rights movements were not far enough backstage in the new shift of the movement.

The tensions Black women felt in the Black liberation movement led them, much like those in the first wave, to organize outside of the objectification they faced within the movement. One such organization that formed was the Third World Women's Alliance (TWWA). Formed in 1968 by Frances

Beale and other women involved with SNCC, the organization "established the early concept of Black feminist organizing as intersectional, with Black women constituting a "vanguard center" whose liberation would mean the liberation of all" (Roth, 2004, p. 91). Roth (2004, p. 77) contends, "Black feminists constructed an ideology of liberation from racial, sexual and class oppression" which she calls a "vanguard center." The formation of Black women's organizations and "consciousness raising" groups represent a collective activism against misogyny (Taylor, 1998, p. 245).

Previous discussion emphasized misogynoir in terms of Black male chauvinism; however, it is also critical to identify misogynoir from white feminist spaces and movements. Frances Beale, leader of TWWA, situates the organization as a think tank and action group in her seminal essay "Double Jeopardy: To Be Black and Female" (Taylor, 1998). Also, within this classic essay Beale highlights the double burden of race and gender that Black women face, as well as the need for white women's liberation efforts to be anti-capitalist and anti-racist. Beale outlined the need to eliminate all forms of oppression to bring about a "new world" that was free for all individuals (Giddings, 1984). Her admonishment of white women's liberation as racist can be seen in an interaction during the Liberation Day March to commemorate the fiftieth anniversary of the Nineteenth Amendment held by the National Women's Organization (NOW). Beale and other members of TWWA held up signs about Angela Davis who had recently been expelled from her position at the University of California and was on the FBI Ten Most Wanted list after being (falsely) charged with first-degree murder, first degree kidnapping and conspiracy to commit both (Giddings, 1984). The women of TWWA were concerned about the wellbeing of Davis considering the climate for Black radicals at the time. However, white women at the march did not share in this concern with Beale claiming that one of the leaders of NOW stated "Angela Davis has nothing to do with the women's liberation" (Giddings, 1984; Taylor, 1998).

In addition to the challenges of Black male chauvinism, Black women also felt alienated by the mainstream women's liberation movement. Taylor (1998) links the women's liberation movement to the freedom summer of 1964, the Civil Rights Act of 1964 and Title VII. Further, the publication of Betty Friedan's *Feminine Mystique* (1963) is said to have "added fuel to the fire of a growing feminist discontent" (Giddings, 1984, p. 299). Freidan's text outlined the issues of middle-class white women, living in suburbia, and seeking to work outside of the home. Her contentions of the disconnect between being a mother and working outside the home—playing her own part in the world—did not register for Black women that had long been disqualified from the cult of true (white) womanhood. Giddings (1984, p. 306) states that the daughters of the women Friedan wrote about joined feminist organizations, particularly NOW, searching to uncover "the meaning of feminism in their personal lives and personal relationships" as opposed to being concerned with the larger political and economic issues of the times. Scholars note that many of the women that joined NOW were white-collar and clerical workers or suburban housewives. Toni Morrison, noted author and Black feminist writer, explained that many Black women saw white women as no less culpable for racism in this country than white men, and pointed to the fact that many of the women who expressed a need to establish herself outside of the house could do so because of the women of color who tended their homes as housekeepers.

Overall, Black women lacked trust for the women's movement due to the reminiscent nature of past movements and organizations that deliberately enrolled Black participation, to simply advance their interests. Larue (1970, p. 37) advances this point noting, "One can argue that women's liberation has not only attached itself to the black movement but has done so with only marginal concern for black women and Black liberation and functional concern for the rights of white women." Furthermore, Giddings (1984) outlines that Black women expressed ambivalence about the women's liberation movement for three main reasons. First, they noted that their experiences did not align with the type of women at the forefront of the movement. Second, the rise of the women's liberation movement coincides with the decline of the civil rights and Black power movements, and finally white women's stance that male supremacy was the root of oppression as opposed to understanding the dialectical nature of oppression was problematic for Black women who also suffered under white supremacy and the economic system.

Essentially, Black women saw white women in the second wave of women's movement as following the traditions of their foremothers, developing their feminism in a movement to end racial injustice, and then ultimately moving on to create organizations that served their interests as white, predominantly middle-class women. Similar to the Black liberation movement, Black women's discontent with the mainstream women's liberation movement led Black women to engage in activism and create organizations that dealt with their unique needs. One such organization was the National Black Feminist Organization (NFBO) established in 1973. The organization is recognized as the most ambitious attempt around Black feminist organizing up until that point, and highlights the need for feminism that Black women saw despite their contentions with the mainstream feminist movement. The Black women within the organization viewed their mission as remedying the idea that women's liberation was irrelevant to Black women, and separate from Black liberation (Roth, 2004). Although the organization was short-lived, it is credited as leading to the formation of one of the most prolific Black feminist organizations in history, The Combahee River Collective.

The Combahee River Collective was formed in 1975 from the Boston chapter of the NBFO to incorporate more radical organizing on behalf of Black women that incorporated a discussion of sexual politics. The collective took its name from the guerrilla foray led by Harriet Tubman, which freed hundreds of enslaved people and was the first and only military campaign in the US planned and executed by a woman (James & Sharpley-Whiting, 2000). In 1977 the collective released its Black feminist manifesto which, much like Frances Beale had done, emphasized the simultaneity of race, gender, heterosexist, and class oppression in the lives of Black women and other women of color, and highlighted their connection to the activist traditions of Black feminism in the 19th century and 1960s (Guy-Sheftall, 1995). The collective is held as one of the truly revolutionary Black feminist organizations, bringing attention to the homophobia within the Black community and carving a space for the recognition of Black lesbians.

One of the most prolific Black feminist lesbian writers was Audre Lorde, who challenged heterosexist practices within the Black and feminist communities, citing that they had the tendency to silence and marginalize lesbians of color. Her collection of essays, *Sister Outsider: Essays and Speeches* (1984) has come to be one of the most critical books on Black feminist consciousness. The works of Lorde and scholars such as bell hooks, and Patricia Hill Collins in the 1980s and 1990s also sought to move Black feminism from the margins to the center of feminist discourse, situating it as a theory and developing a continuous Black feminist intellectual tradition. Lorde's work with storytelling has perhaps made one of the most lasting impacts on the way we shape, frame and tell our story in this book. Its connections to Black feminism and critiques of white feminist spaces have given us the courage to share our stories collectively.

Feminism in the Late 20th Century: Black Feminist Theory in the Academy

Feminism as an area of scholastic inquiry has been a part of higher education for as long as women have been a part of higher education. Still, influenced by student activists who demanded Black studies programs, the first women's studies departments did not emerge until the 1970s and 1980s when small, interdisciplinary programs began cropping up around the United States. In these first few decades, academics would grapple with questions about who and what should fall under the purview of "women's studies" (Boxer, 1998). Many, especially in the public mainstream media, believed women's studies should remain completely divorced from the academy, citing concerns about how higher education would dilute the inherent political nature of feminism. In those spaces where feminism was integrated into the academy, it tended to mirror the most oppressive aspects of "mainstream" feminist organizing and, in most instances, women's studies departments simply provided the most "accomplished" racist and classist women a greater reach and a wider audience (Walkington, 2017). The 1980s and 1990s were supposed to have been a great "turning point" for academic feminists (Mohanty, 1989). This supposed turning point is referred to as "third wave" feminism, a new brand of feminism said to be more inclusive of women of color specifically.

This third wave is also commonly thought of as the moment when intersectional feminism becomes dominant because it is at this time, we see a great deal of Black women writers gaining notoriety. They saw the importance of demonstrating their reality through writing and distributing their work in an effort to speak for themselves (Guy-Sheftall, 1995). These efforts culminated in public discourse about Black women and feminist theory, even resulting in Kitchen Table: Women of Color Press, founded by Black feminist scholars Audre Lorde and Barbara Smith, with the mission of publishing feminist scholarship by women of color (Guy-Sheftall, 1995). This collective scholarship—which also consists of highlighting the scholarship of Black women in the eras before—expressed something in addition to the collective standpoint Black women engaged in through feminist efforts. According to Collins (1989, p. 750):

> Black feminist thought represents a second level of knowledge, furnished by experts who are part of a group and who express the groups standpoint...black feminist thought articulates the taken for granted knowledge of African American women, it

also encourages all black women to create new self-definitions that validate a black women's standpoint.

Just a few years earlier, hooks made a similar argument, noting the importance of developing theoretical frameworks about power and inequality out of the lived experience of those on the margins of feminist movement (hooks 1984). In her text *Ain't I a Woman: Black Women and Feminism* (1981) she discussed the impact of sexism on the lives of Black women at length and defended feminist ideology, while simultaneously providing critiques of white feminism. Further, in her text *Feminist Theory: From Margin to Center* (1984), she again critiques feminism for simply assessing inequality between the sexes as opposed to the "ideology of domination" that supports inequality in general. Put simply, racism and sexism equal power, privilege and control. Specifically in the essay "Black Women: Shaping Feminist Theory" she outlines her own issues with feminism and asserts that Black women have a unique position through our lived experience that makes us most able to challenge various dominant ideologies, and contribute significantly to feminist theory (hooks, 1984), a unique position we share in subsequent chapters.

Patricia Hill Collins sought to articulate the collective consciousness that Black women have been demonstrating throughout history with their activism and scholarship. Her landmark book *Black Feminist Thought* (1990) outlined the connection of activism and theory in the lives of Black women. Collins outlines core themes that can be seen in the lived experience of Black women forming a collective standpoint—the interconnectedness of race, class and gender oppression in Black women's lives; the need to reject typical stereotypes of Black women and internalize positive self-images; and the importance of active struggle to resist oppression and realize individual as well as group empowerment (Collins, 2000). Collins contends that Black feminist theory is necessary—despite its suppression within and outside of the academy—because "social theories emerging from and/or on behalf of Black women and other historically oppressed groups aim to find ways to escape from service in, and/or oppose prevailing social and economic injustice" (2000, p. 11). Following Collins's theorizing, Black women intellectuals seek to reclaim Black women's subjugated knowledge, and highlight Black women's collective standpoint, as we argue in *The Black Feminist Coup*. While Collins is careful to note that there is no one homogenous standpoint, rather "the Black *women's* collective standpoint is characterized by the tensions that accrue to different responses to common challenges" (2000, p. 32).

A range of factors combined to construct the narrative that the impending new millennium would mark a time of great transformation, equity, and inclusion for feminism and the publication of Kimberlé Crenshaw's article "Demarginalizing the Intersection of Race and Sex" (1989) was absolutely a contributing factor. In this seminal piece, Crenshaw formally introduces academics to the concept of intersectionality and the response is a resounding "Yes, see! Feminists are now woke!" Since then, academics across several disciplines have been prolific in their application of the term both in their teaching and research (see Collins, 2015; Potter, 2015). In many ways, Crenshaw's application of the term intersectionality provided a frame with which academics could understand the lives of doubly and triply marginalized people (on their terms), possibly for the first time.

Crenshaw's piece is often pointed to as evidence that feminists were beginning to think of gender as a system implicated by other identities and is commonly used as a starting point to trace Black women's contribution to feminist theorizing (Potter, 2015). Since "Demarginalizing the Intersection of Race and Sex," intersectionality and intersectional research have become a fixture within feminist studies and academic research in general (Collins, 2015; Roth, 2017; Thatcher et al., 2023). According to Vivian E. May (2015), feminists tend to view the institutionalization of intersectionality as an indication of widespread acceptance of Black women within feminist movement and scholarship. Our experiences shared in this book indicate that quick acceptance of intersectionality is not actually an indication of feminists engaging with Black women's theorizing.

Existing research in this area highlights a concern among women of color scholars regarding the institutionalization of intersectionality. Knapp (2005) believes theories like intersectionality that travel quickly through the academy often gain acceptance at the cost of losing their original intent and critical edge. Nikol Alexander-Floyd (2012) discusses how critical perspectives born out of Black feminism are weakened as they become further entrenched in institutionalized spaces. Chandra Mohanty (2003), a transnational feminist scholar, discusses how her work on intersectional feminism has been "misappropriated" in the academy and misrepresented. Bilge (2013) examines how intersectionality has become "depoliticized" and "whitened" and used to do no more than take inventory of peoples' privileged and oppressed identities. Ness (2010) makes a similar argument, pointing out how feminist researchers often claim they are using intersectionality on girls and women but fail to treat racial and class identities as interconnected products of social hierarchies. These intersectionality scholars are thus making the argument that for something to be truly intersectional there must be, as bell hooks has argued, a critical analysis of power as a multi-dimensional force that shares a dialectical relationship with the social identities they are tied to. Put simply, intersectionality must go beyond merely recognizing that individuals are both gendered and raced (Arnold, 1990).

In her second article, "Mapping the Margins" (1991) Kimberlé Crenshaw addresses this very issue. Realizing that her perspective was being used in analyses of identity void of any discussion of power, Crenshaw pushed people who lay claim to intersectionality to recognize that identities are more than mere descriptive categories—they are socially constructed and politically and culturally negotiated. Time does not seem to have been helpful in changing the way intersectionality has been handled, however. In a 2014 interview, Kimberlé Crenshaw was quoted saying, intersectionality has a "wide reach, but not [a] very deep one: it is both over- and underused; sometimes I can't even recognize it in the literature anymore" (Carastathis, 2014). Collins (2015) speaks further to the de-politicization of intersectionality she encountered at a women's festival in South America: "They were surprised by my argument that US Black feminism and intersectionality were interconnected knowledge projects, stating bluntly, "We thought intersectionality was for white feminists and that it had nothing to do with us" (p. 15).

Clearly, there is widespread belief that intersectionality has been adopted by whites within feminism. For intersectionality to be meaningfully adopted, one must recognize that systems of power constantly interact with one another in significant ways (Crenshaw, 1989, 1991) that stratify women differentially and enable some of us to exercise power over others (hooks, 1984; Levine-Raskey, 2011). As we will share through our stories, it is the co-opting of intersectionality in pursuit of a selfish agenda which led us to realize that our only option was to leave the Department of Gender and Women's Studies.

Mainstream white feminist theorizing merely erases the significance of race such that white feminists are not required to engage with the reality of racial stratification in the United States (Moreton-Robinson, 2000). Put simply, for intersectionality to be meaningfully adopted by feminists, whiteness (along with other privilege categories) must be recognized as a relevant variable in experience with sexism, as we argue in subsequent chapters. In the absence of this recognition, white feminists cannot claim to be intersectional. Intersectionality cannot co-exist with unexamined privilege because power left unexamined is power maintained (Frankenberg, 1993; hooks, 2000a; Lugones, 2003; Ortega, 2006; Levine-Raskey, 2011; DiAngelo, 2011, 2018).

Conclusion

As readers will see in the stories we share in subsequent chapters, the erasure of Black women's contributions continues to be an issue in feminist spaces. We were silenced and marginalized: the Department of Gender and Women's Studies, white feminists, and self-proclaimed allies feigned diversity and inclusion politics even though their actions spoke differently. Further when institutions finally started paying attention to their impacts on Black lives, many white feminists aimed to co-opt and appropriate that struggle for their own personal gain.

Storytelling and truth-telling, as Black women and co-conspirators (Ekpe & Toutant, 2022), come with significant consequences. In telling our stories, particularly for those of us pre-tenured (Olivia and Jennifer), we recognize the potential for retaliation and negative future interactions with those we hold accountable here. In fact, each of us must contend with the possibilities of being labeled and treated as "troublemakers," "liars," or "unprofessional." As Yarbrough and Bennett (2000) remind us in "Cassandra and the 'Sistahs': the Peculiar Treatment of African American Women in the Myth of Women as Liars," (2000) Black women are often viewed with three types of stereotypical myths: (1) the mammy, as discussed later in this book, (2) the jezebel, and (3) the sapphire (p. 639). Yarbrough and Bennett describe "cassandra," specifically as a sibling of jezebel: While jezebel is described as promiscuous Black women who are to be "tamed and possessed" (p. 640), the "Cassandra myth is often referred to as a simple tale of a mortal woman refusing the advances of a god and suffering the consequences: a clear vision of the future in which no one would believe" (p. 640). The key ideas representative of the "Cassandra Myth" include resistance, mortality (succumbing to consequences), and a lack of belief in Black women. Put simply, when Black women resist oppression, we suffer the consequences, and when we speak out as victims of oppression, we are not believed.

For us, like many before us, we run the risk of not only our stories not being believed, but also the consequences in telling them. For Mariam, she withheld drafts of this manuscript from her promotion to full professor file in fear of retaliation consequences. After Staci, Jennifer and Mariam (2022) previously published an article describing our exodus from the Department of Gender and Women's Studies ("A Time to Dream"), Staci and Mariam were contacted by a GWS faculty member and interrogated about whether we were talking about them negatively in the article. Furthermore, we also acknowledge that for Olivia, her white allyship or accomplice-ness, comes at a price as she could be labeled and treated as a "race-traitor." Nonetheless, these stories are too important, and we cannot be held hostage to possible consequences.

· 3 ·

MARIAM'S STORY
NOT IN MY NAME: HARM, ACCOUNTABILITY, AND TRANSFORMATIVE JUSTICE IN GENDER AND WOMEN'S STUDIES

I have two experiences about my tenure at my institution to tell you about. The first one is about the Africana Studies program, and the second one is about my experience in the Department of Gender and Women's Studies. As readers will find, they are interconnected and woven, as I began in one department, moved to another, and now I have returned home to the unit now called The Institute for Intercultural and Anthropological Studies (IIAS). IIAS now houses the African American and African Studies Program. By sharing this story, I reveal the intersectionality between race and gender, and the ways in which white feminism has impeded progress with respect to both Gender and Women's Studies and African American and African Studies.

How It Began: A Teacher-Scholar of Africana Studies Courted by Gender and Women's Studies

In the fall of 2007, I joined the Africana Studies (AFS) Program as the first female tenure-track faculty to be hired in over a decade. Then in the spring of 2010, there was an interpersonal incident between one of the faculty members and the Director of AFS. The faculty member accused the Director of yelling at him and slapping him. The incident led to the campus police being called as a result of the alleged physical assault. As a result, the university chapter of the American Association of University Professors (AAUP) Union (our institution's collective bargaining agent) and the College of Arts and Sciences (CAS) administration were consulted to take action, and eventually a civil lawsuit ensued based on the alleged assault. This incident ultimately led to the Director stepping down and his forced transfer to the department of History. Without a director, the future of AFS was put in peril.

In the fall of 2011, Associate Dean, M. Ann told me that there were not enough faculty members to teach AFS courses. (Later in this chapter, I discuss M. Ann's role as one of the Gender and Women's Studies Department colleagues responsible for the department's toxicity.) Meanwhile, I was serving as the academic advisor for AFS minors and majors. Associate Dean M. Ann told me to focus on making sure that students who were already pursuing a minor or major in AFS graduated and not to enroll any new students in the program. I was to direct any new students interested in AFS to the CAS Advising Office. The AFS program was "suspended" (put under "Review") and put under the dean of the CAS receivership. This meant that control of the department would now be moved under the college, as opposed to an AFS director and faculty. Also, only one AFS introduction course would be taught. Through the grapevine, I later learned that all our prospective students were being sent to another unit, which housed a race and ethnic relations minor instead, and not Africana Studies.

According to Associate Dean M. Ann, the reason why "there were not enough faculty members to teach AFS courses" was because of the sudden retirement of one of the faculty members; a sudden retirement that I think was a result of him being pushed out by the CAS Dean's Office after they determined that he was too "problematic" to handle. I also believe that Associate Dean M. Ann, who "suspended" The Africana Studies Program, saw the AFS as a constant threat to GWS. She was previously the director of the then Women's Studies Program [WMS], which would later be named the Department of Gender and Women's Studies. She wanted to neutralize the threat by no longer having GWS "share" the Administrative Assistant who had served the AFS for more than a decade. Additionally, she endeavored to take over the offices and space for GWS that used to be those occupied by AFS.

I must also note that in her zeal to grow the WMS program, M. Ann had been courting me for over two years to join the WMS program but to no avail. During that time she was serving as an associate dean of the College of Arts and Sciences (CAS). Eventually, WMS officially became the Department of Gender and Women's Studies (GWS). After several failed attempts, M. Ann called me into her office to try to convince me to send in my transfer request from AFS before another faculty member's transfer to GWS. Prior to that conversation with her, I had no knowledge of the identity of the other faculty member. I suspect that, by putting AFS under the receivership of CAS and suspending all new enrollments to the program, the writing was on the wall and I too, was forced to make a decision between joining GWS or being pushed out altogether. I felt like I could no longer keep my job if I stayed in a program that had been "suspended." The only choice left to me was to move to GWS.

Thus, feeling caught between a rock and a hard place, I reluctantly decided to join GWS in the fall of 2012, a place in which many Black feminists before me have been caught when being forced to make decisions based on race versus gender. So much for intersectionality. However, the official reasons given for the suspension of the program were not adding up. Previously, AFS faculty were told that admission to the Africana Studies Program had been suspended pending a review of the curriculum, but the curricular review never happened. I was determined to fight for the reinstatement of the AFS program as a GWS faculty member.

Toxicity: White Feminists and GWS

My hunch about GWS' toxicity and M. Ann's plotting to suspend AFS had been right. I felt cornered and defeated because that was the only option; I had to keep my job since the AFS program had been "suspended" indefinitely. One of the reasons I was reluctant to join GWS was because in the previous years when M. Ann was the director of the Women's Studies Program, she undertook steps to completely rid the department of all part-time instructors that she did not like. I saw how she treated people who stood up to her and how she was bad mouthing colleagues from other units who wanted to transfer to GWS. It was clear that M. Ann would get rid of anyone she did not like, or anyone she saw as a "troublemaker." For instance, in Jennifer's narrative, readers will see how she would come for other colleagues—Gloria, Reba, Jennifer, Becca, and me, all feminist faculty in GWS.

What happened to us in Gender and Women's Studies was the result of prolonged indifference and years of accumulated complicity from administrators who were supposed to provide a healthy work environment for employees. Apparently, institutional systems were in place that made it possible for a few people to cause so much harm to their co-workers with impunity. Some of us sought help from and notified the CAS's Dean's office, which had just hired a new dean in 2016. Her role will be discussed later in this book. In 2017, we also solicited support from the Office of Diversity and Inclusion, as well as the local AAUP chapter. We hoped to share and seek solutions to some of the issues we were experiencing with our departmental leadership under the department chair, Karen (M. Ann's partner), and M. Ann, who had resigned her post as associate dean before returning to the GWS department as a faculty member. It wasn't until October 2020, that a new provost recognized all of the harm previously done and made the decision to move us into a new unit. That said, concerns about accountability and unresolved consequences would continue.

During the time that M. Ann served as the Associate Dean in the CAS, she fought to have Karen automatically become the chair of GWS when it transitioned to the Gender and Women's Studies Department. When Karen became chair, she ruled the unit with an iron fist, although I was in M. Ann and Karen's good graces as long as I was the quiet, submissive, "playing nice in the sandbox," African woman. Karen was not very collegial and was very rigid on her principles. For example, when I was preparing my portfolio for my tenure promotion, I asked her if she could print out about four heading pages in color on her office printer, since my printer only printed in black and white. To my dismay, Karen told me that I could go to Kinkos off campus to print my pages. I was dumbfounded by her lack of goodwill. This was the very first time I had ever asked her for such a favor, and for her to blatantly refuse to do me that favor, as if I had been taking advantage of her, was shocking. Usually, chairs are supportive of their faculty, especially as they prepare documents for tenure and promotion. Instead, Karen told me she did not want to set a precedent where I assumed I could always have her print stuff out for me.

Interpersonal issues started to emerge more in GWS in 2015–2016 during our departmental meetings. The obvious nepotism that resulted from Karen being M. Ann's partner laid the groundwork for the beginning of the toxic environment to come. Things became especially tense when Reba and Gloria, two white colleagues in the department, asked Karen pertinent questions about the budget or informed Karen that she could not ask faculty to attend faculty retreats before the official fall calendar started, as suggested by our institution's collective bargaining agreement. I guess Karen took Reba's and Gloria's questions as challenges to her power. Both Karen and M. Ann started to have intense "arguments" during our departmental meetings. Sometimes, the debates on both sides got so heated, and information to which I was not privy during any of our meetings was disclosed so many times that I started to think: There has to be a backstory to these arguments. And come to find out, there was! Reba felt and told Karen that, as chair, Karen was not open to criticism and that she was leading the unit as a tyrant. Reba eventually left the department due to their hostility and transferred to the Sociology Department at the end of the spring semester in 2016.

Karen's Third Term as Chair: More White Feminist Toxicity

In the spring of 2017, Karen's second term as a chair was up, although we assumed she was vying for a third term. As a white woman who often touted campus initiatives on gender equity, the current CAS dean asked us to send in our nominations for the new chair. Karen and M. Ann told us to send votes to the department assistant that would then be sent to the dean. The names of Karen and Becca (a self-proclaimed "ally") were the two candidates sent to the Dean. The Dean asked us for individual feedback regarding the strengths and weaknesses of both Becca and Karen. After the faculty voted on the next chair, the Dean met with me individually. During that meeting I told her that in the spirit of fairness and shared governance, I would rather see Becca become chair. I also told her that Karen's leadership had been very controversial and created division within the department. She then sent me an email asking to meet again.

When I went to that meeting, the Dean asked me if I wanted to be the chair of GWS, which came as a total shock. She told me that I was a better fit for the position and that my tempered nature would calm the volatile situation in GWS and bring some sort of much needed healing to the department. This was a blatant reinforcement of a stereotype that being a calm and reserved African woman makes me "more palatable" and thus an asset for leadership. I politely declined her offer to step into the role of department chair, as I was not interested in taking on the additional stress the politics and toxic culture of the department embodied. At the end of our meeting, she told me that if I were to change my mind, I should let her know. I was shocked that she would not consider the two candidates who wanted to serve as chair and asked me to step into that role instead.

I had hoped that after serving two consecutive three-year terms as chair, Karen would be gracious enough to let Becca serve in the spirit of shared governance. However, by the spring of 2017, both Karen and M. Ann felt that GWS was their baby and that only they were entitled to chair it. Despite the fact that Jennifer, Becca, Gloria, and I voiced our concerns about Karen's lack of shared governance and abuse of power, the Dean still went ahead and reappointed her for a third term! We were all devastated! But of course, I understood what was going on. I felt like the Dean was simply virtue signaling diversity by offering me the position, but did not really care about how we felt, and it also seemed that gender equity applied exclusively to white women. I also knew that Karen would retaliate once she found out that we voted for Becca. We knew that we had to brace for a fallout once the fall 2017 semester started.

There was already an unfriendly, resentful, and hostile environment at the time Karen was reappointed as chair in the spring of 2017. It often seems as though Black women are expected to demonstrate loyalty and pick sides; feminist solidarity that is never reciprocated. Ultimately, there were two distinct camps in the department: Karen and M. Ann in one camp and Gloria, Jennifer, Becca, and I in the other, clearly reflecting the expectation that Black women must pick sides with regard to feminism. Shortly thereafter in August 2017, Gloria, Jennifer, Becca, and I realized that the result of the GWS chair election was miscounted. We reported it to the Dean in a formal letter in which we copied the director of the Office of Institutional Equity (OIE). We also told the dean in another email that we sent her on August 25, 2017, that we simply wished to resolve the problems that made our work-environment unpleasant and untrusting, and affected our ability to function as a unified body under Karen's leadership. We added that we would like to meet with the Dean in order for her to mediate a department discussion. Initially the Dean agreed to this meeting.

By this time, Karen started to discredit us by defaming our character. She spread several rumors about us. One of them was that Becca, Jennifer, and I have created a "single story" of solely blaming Karen for the problems in GWS. Starting in the fall of 2017, Karen also started to retaliate against us for questioning her reappointment process. She galvanized the GWS Advisory Board members, who were all her personal friends, to show up at every single one of our departmental meetings, even though most of them were not board-appointed faculty in GWS. Their constant presence prevented us from bringing up our internal issues during our departmental meetings. As a result, we felt very uncomfortable and could not openly discuss interpersonal issues related to our department in their presence.

Thus, I sent Karen an email asking her to set aside a faculty meeting for just us, the core GWS faculty, so that we could feel free to bring up some of the issues we had with her and find a resolution. Karen refused to do so. She used the GWS Advisory Board as a shield against us. This too, became a power struggle. The entire department (with the exception of Karen and M. Ann) were very unhappy as we felt that she created a hostile and stressful working environment for us. Karen told us that if we felt that she had violated any university rule, then we should file a complaint with the Office of Institutional Equity (OIE). Although the Dean had initially agreed, she decided not to meet with us as a group, and rather instructed us to work things out with Karen and M. Ann on our own for reasons we could only speculate. That ended the oversight and consultation from the Dean's office.

There is no doubt that M. Ann and Karen created an atmosphere in the department that suppressed and punished dissent. They also pushed those who disagreed with them to feel so uncomfortable that they decided to transfer to other departments (as in the case of Reba, Gloria, and Jennifer Richardson). M. Ann was also ready to punish any faculty who challenged the way Karen ran the department. This is well illustrated in an email that M. Ann sent to me on May 2, 2017 fishing for information regarding to Gloria:

> I tried for years to reach out to *my difficult colleagues*, but a few of them had already made up their minds. Period. They didn't simply disagree with me, but made it clear that they despised me and felt unapologetically entitled to treat me with disdain. ...
> As I said, though, I am actually pretty optimistic right now precisely because some unhappy folks have moved on to homes that may fit them better. I have confidence that the rest of us can leave this behind us and look to the future so long as we are all clear about the need to behave *like professionals and like adults* (emphasis added).

After receiving several emails like this from M. Ann over the years, I came to the realization that because I wasn't outspoken about what was going on in the department (up to that point), this was her way of "taking me to the side" to pump me for information and possibly manipulate me into her side as she controlled the narrative. Although I did respond to her email over a week later, I did not give her the response she was looking for as I saw what she was doing. I just reiterated to her the importance of maintaining professionalism, collegiality, and respect for each other at all times.

By the beginning of spring 2018 Jennifer, Becca, and I were so tired of complaining to no avail that we resigned ourselves to just endure the hostile environment. I told myself that I would not care anymore; that I would just go and teach my classes and go home. I felt defeated, but that was the only way I could keep my sanity. While the atmosphere in the department seemed civil on the surface, hurt feelings and distrust continued. We were divided more than ever. In the fall of 2018, after taking a sick leave that was approved by Human Resources (HR), Karen tried to retaliate against me by assigning me an additional course to teach in the spring of 2019, instead of my regular two courses. Her explanation for assigning me three courses was that I did not teach during the fall as a result of taking a leave of absence, to which I was entitled for a Family and Medical Leave (FMLA). I had to go through the university AAUP, which threatened to grieve Karen's punitive decision to get her to back off. There were several email correspondences between an AAUP Union Grievance Officer and me regarding this situation. Karen finally backed off and we came to an agreement that after my sick leave was over, that my work for the remainder of the semester would fall under a Latinx woman who was serving as the interim director of the newly formed Institute for Intercultural and Anthropological Studies (IIAS) instead. I was bracing myself for more retaliatory behavior from Karen in the fall of 2018, as the situation in the department continued to be very tense, and everyone was walking on eggshells. The department was more divided than ever.

2020: When All Hell and White Supremacy Broke Loose Everywhere!

In the spring of 2020, Karen's third term was up. It was time for GWS to go through the process of nominating a new department chair once again. Every faculty member in the department could either self-nominate, or nominate a colleague to be chair. After being encouraged and supported by the Dean to enroll in a year-long leadership academy, once more Becca emerged as one of the candidates. Nevertheless, M. Ann sabotaged the process by nominating everyone else but Becca, Staci, Jennifer, Bella (a new joint-appointed GWS faculty hire), and me. I believe this is because she knew the other joint-appointed faculty would either support her or Karen (due to their friendships and alliances with both of them), and not Becca (since one of the joint appointees regularly communicated about Becca's toxicity while serving as a colleague in Becca's former department); hence, most of the joint appointed faculty she nominated declined. Only one of them accepted her nomination.

When the pandemic hit, the Dean was hesitant to appoint a chair, not only because of the economic crisis, but also, we assume, as a way to resolve the toxic environment in the department. At this point, M. Ann started to spread rumors nationally and across campus about the Dean's unwillingness to appoint a chair and the divestment of GWS by the CAS and our institution as a whole. She and Karen turned the department into a platform of criticism of the Dean and the Provost and ignited a national campaign to bring attention to the false claim that our institution intended to get rid of the GWS department by refusing to nominate a chair. Letters and petitions flooded the Dean's, Provost's and President's offices. During the same time period, in the midst of a pandemic and televised killing of George Floyd, the dysfunctional, stressful and hostile work environment in GWS kept getting worse and worse by the day. The drama seemed endless.

Following George Floyd's murder and the anti-Blackness events that ensued, Black people in this country were on the edge. We were stressed and tired of the senseless killings of our people. Karen and M. Ann, now joined by Rachel (a new colleague-- who transferred in from another department-- eager to team up with Karen and M. Ann), kept bombarding us with emails that were focused solely on garnishing support of all faculty (Becca, Bella, Jennifer, and me) to join the campaign for the appointment of a GWS chair, while completely paying no attention to the anti-Blackness sentiment that the country was experiencing. Karen and M. Ann would use Black women as a token just to serve their own interests, while showing no empathy or care whatsoever for their Black and Brown colleagues. So, even though we were supposed to be on summer vacation, they kept sending us email after email showing that their primary and only concern was for the Dean to appoint a chair and, in my opinion, ensure that it was not Becca. It seemed that they felt Becca was not suited to lead the department.

During this time, they ignored invitations to events Jennifer and I shared with them pertaining to white allyship with Black women. When we brought that to their attention, M. Ann would start a new email thread that focused on the issue of the chair appointment, just to avoid responding to the concerns about their lack of concern, care and empathy that we women of color were getting from our white colleagues. Jennifer and Staci also shared concerns about M. Ann's and Karen's lack of empathy, but to no avail. In addition, despite the fact that on two occasions in early June, I personally shared emails with the entire faculty stating that Karen and M. Ann's emails were heightening our anxieties. Bella, another LatinX faculty member in GWS, also disclosed that the situation led her to seek professional help for her mental health. Despite all of this, Karen and M. Ann upped the ante and showed a complete lack of respect and consideration to our concerns as Black and Brown women:

> Hi all,
>
> I understand that everyone's focus is pulled in lots of directions right now, given the national catastrophe and its hideous escalation of violence against Black Americans in particular. The threat levels we are experiencing—especially our colleagues of color—are unprecedented, made all the worse by the pandemic and economic insecurity that has resulted from our nation's failed leadership.
>
> And then there's [our current institution]. I believe that our collective struggle to retain a fully resourced Department of Gender and Women's Studies is as important as ever while we witness emboldened anti-Black racism and an increasingly authoritarian federal government. Holding ... leadership to account to make equitable decisions is as important as ever. As you know, the lives and careers trajectories of all our faculty—one of the most racially diverse academic units in CAS—are at stake here. For us, and for our students, staff, and faculty, our mission continues to be one of education, research, and advocacy that centers marginalized people and communities and questions abuse of power. In the context of organized and militarized state violence that upholds white supremacy, our department makes a relatively small contribution, but it is nevertheless one that advances social justice and affects the lives of many.
>
> I say this in advance of sending you all a separate email about the messages from administration that continue to threaten our department's viability and autonomy. Those of us with the privilege (white skin or otherwise) and capacity to engage with [our institution's] power structures is essential in this moment.
>
> And besides holding power accountable, there is also the work of supporting marginalized members of our community. Each of us is likely to be drawn to do different things. In terms of our students and others who care about GWS, I will plan to reach out to them soon—and if you desire to act or speak collectively, please weigh in. Karen

A second email shows the same pattern that Karen had of co-opting anti-racism in the service of preserving her tenure legacy in GWS. Jennifer and I expressed our displeasure over Karen and M. Ann's tactics with all of our colleagues. This second email was a continuation and justification while actually acknowledging that she was doing the very thing that I had told her was causing harm and anxiety to her Black colleagues:

> Hello, all,
>
> I thank Jennifer for getting this conversation started, and I appreciate Jennifer and Mariam for sharing more explicitly your experiences and perspectives about fear and disappointment. I'm glad others who wish to are weighing in as well. It is a time for holding one another accountable, and people with white privilege (etc.) have extra responsibility to acknowledge and attend to our Black, indigenous, and people of color colleagues and friends. I stand in solidarity with you all, especially Jennifer, Mariam, [Bella], and Staci, and will do my part to collaborate where I can.
>
> It's exciting to see the things that organizations and GWS departments, among others, are doing are to make collective statements and plan resistance events. We in GWS at [our institution] don't have a track record, as a department, of crafting statements or organizing events. Normally summer is a time when… faculty enjoy the peace and freedom to pursue your individual projects and get respite from the grind of meetings, emails, and obligations to the university. But of course I get that times are very different, and I could see how the urgency of current events might lead the department on a new path.
>
> Yes, Mariam, you are right to point out that my communications and efforts have primarily focused on closing out department work that needs to be finished before I end my role as chair. I can see why that is frustrating. The College and University are choosing to disinvest in the security and future of GWS at [our institution], and I remain alarmed about our administrators' actions and the implications for faculty, especially our faculty of color who are most vulnerable. My efforts to build and lead the GWS department over almost a decade are being brought to a sudden halt. The end of my term is not a problem; what is a problem is that I cannot "pass a baton" to a GWS colleague at this time. The dean seems steadfast in her decision to withhold the baton from our department, and her and the provost's messages and recent town halls are driving home the point with utter clarity: our faculty lives will forever be changed in the wake of COVID-19, especially in GWS where our self-governance has been invalidated.
>
> While my days are numbered, I am doing what I can to maintain our department as a tenure home, particularly in service of our colleagues Jennifer and [Bella] who we hired and brought to work in, and earn tenure in, the interdisciplinary field of Gender and Women's Studies. If the GWS department is reduced in stature and status, as appears to be the writing on the wall, if we are farmed out to an associate dean or a

random department chair from another department, or to a conglomerate like the Institute, we will have lost our autonomy and have no reason to believe that it will be restored. I keep pointing out to various decision makers on campus that the security of our untenured faculty—faculty of color—in GWS are harmed by [our institution]'s abandonment of a fully-supported GWS department. Empty reassurances that [our institution's] leadership is committed to equity, diversity, and so on have not satisfied me, and I suspect they aren't much comfort to you all, either.

So in my remaining time in the chair's seat, I am working to minimize the risks that we will be exploited as GWS faculty for excessive teaching assignments. I am trying best I can to ensure some continuity of classes and programs, knowing that our students' lives are transformed in the GWS classroom, and that all of us have invested significant parts of our professional lives into being educators who make a difference for our students.

This work I'm doing is a small piece of resistance, and only an indirect response to the national crisis. I'm sure in this message that I have done the very thing that troubles you, Mariam, and probably others, by continuing to focus on the department's future. I hope I have conveyed why this is where the most of my energy is placed in this unnerving time.

Karen

Although Karen seemed to offer us words of support and solidarity and acknowledge our experiences that I mentioned in my email to her, she immediately followed it with the same invalidation I had pointed out earlier in my email, as she herself has so well noted. She quickly pivoted back to the claim of divestment in GWS.

Karen's email shows that she and M. Ann had fanned much of the fear mongering, as well as gloom and doom scenarios in our department. It also shows a pattern of disregard and a complete lack of care for our well-being. Karen and M. Ann's incessant emails heightened our anxieties, along with other colleagues of color, for whom they professed to care so deeply, and whose names they weaponized to make their points, causing immeasurable psychological damage. They turned a deaf ear to our repeated pleas to stop. At one point, M. Ann even sent a private message to Staci asking her to publicly pledge support for GWS, to which Staci declined, referencing her own mental health concerns. Consequently, M. Ann backed off.

My understanding of gender and women's studies has always been based on the concept that it provides a space where values of feminism such as sisterhood, solidarity, caring, empathy, community, shared vision of liberation, ending racism, discrimination, and accountability are valued and practiced.

For instance, in one of my email responses to Karen's dismissal of our pleas, I stated:

> [Karen], thank you for acknowledging the threat levels that especially, us your colleagues of color are experiencing! However, I feel that the seriousness of that statement tends to get lost because every time that concern was made in an e-mail, the message seemed to underscore more the issue of our GWS Chair crisis than a genuine concern for our well-being per, as faculty of color, particularly during these extremely psychologically taxing times.
>
> I cannot speak for Jen, [Bella] or Staci, but I would have very much appreciated a message of support, of solidarity, and/or just to find out how I am doing from my colleagues who have not yet reached out to me.
>
> Thank you!
>
> Mariam

In presumably feminist spaces, the concept of accountability becomes key to making sure that we hold each other responsible for respecting our shared values. It more importantly involves a sense of being mindful about how our actions can impact others. Accountability is about being responsible for one's choices as well as the consequences for those choices. It means that when someone has caused harm, that person has to answer for their actions.

However, for the last six years, the actions of several of our white feminist colleagues in the Gender and Women's Studies Department had not been in alignment with what I thought were shared feminist core values. Instead, most of our colleagues were using feminism to sanction and legitimize harm. They had been harming us while pretending to advocate in the names of their Black and Brown colleagues. Their agenda was hidden under the cloak of a narrative about a threat of the GWS department being dissolved. Alas, Karen and M. Ann kept deflecting accountability by pretending they did nothing wrong or were unaware that they caused harm. They expected a work environment based on collegiality, without being accountable to those of us they were harming. Karen and M. Ann hijacked external social justice initiatives to claim that gender and women's studies departments were one of few places on campus where Black and Brown bodies mattered. They simultaneously alleged that the GWS curriculum offers Black and Brown people support. In reality, Karen and M. Ann simply wanted to serve as chair, as they felt so entitled to the position. Between the two, they behaved as if only they could chair the department. They showed neither grace, nor a sense of shared governance towards their colleagues.

Karen and M. Ann did not care about any change in the harm and anti-Blackness that was targeting Blacks. Neither did they care about the mental health of their own Black and Brown colleagues who had to endure not only the daily trauma of seeing Blacks die as a result of police brutality, but the continued harm caused by white colleagues who heightened our anxieties by weaving false narratives about the dismantling of GWS and the eventual loss of our jobs. Further, nominating a chair and making sure that a GWS department survives can in no way be compared to the dehumanizing police brutality that Black and Brown people were experiencing. Such a comparison made it clear that our white colleagues "were not revealing an awareness of or sensitivity to [our] lot; they were simply appropriating the horror of [Black people's] experience to enhance their own cause...precisely because white women wanted to see no change in the social status of blacks until they were assured that their demands for more rights were met" (hooks, 1981, p. 126).

Our white colleagues used their white privilege and social status on campus and in society to draw national attention to the false narrative of the plight of a GWS department. By so doing, they acted "as if feminist ideology existed solely to serve their own interests because they were able to draw public attention to feminist concerns" (hooks, 1981, p. 137). These women did not care to acknowledge the ways in which their own racially-charged and privileged behaviors were harming us. And even when we brought it to their attention and asked them to stop, they kept doubling down. Rachel, and Becca responded by sending Jennifer, Bella and me emails away from M. Ann and Karen's eyes, offering shallow platitudes of how they too were hurt by the racial unrest. Karen and M. Ann ultimately enrolled all white women in the department in being more concerned about ensuring their power position in the racial and social hierarchy than worrying about the dire circumstances their Black and brown colleagues were in, therefore offering yet another example of how they co-opted commitments to social justice.

Our white colleagues' lack of acknowledgment of Black women's issues meant that racism is a problem that only concerns Blacks, and as such, it is our issue to deal with. As Lorde (1983/2018) reminds us:

> Advocating the mere tolerance of differences between women is the grossest reformism. It is the total denial of the creative function of difference in our lives. Difference must not be merely tolerated, but seen as a fund of necessary polarities between which our creativity can spark like a dialectic. Only then does the necessity for interdependency become unthreatening. Only within that interdependency of different strengths, acknowledged and equal, can the power to seek new ways of being in the

world be generated, as well as the courage and sustenance to act where there are no charters. Within the interdependence of mutual (nondominant) differences lies that security which enables us to descend into the chaos of knowledge and return with true visions of our future, along with the concomitant power to effect those changes which can bring that future into being. Difference is that raw and powerful connection from which our personal power is forged (pp. 111–112).

The GWS department "tolerated difference" in order to court us to grow the number of faculty in their department; however, I would soon realize that I needed to flee this chaos and return to a new home, one that would house the same program where I was initially hired at our institution.

As a result of these experiences in summer 2020, Jennifer and I sent a well-documented complaint to OIE and the Office of Diversity and Inclusion, asking for institutional support. Although we felt that our work environment was very toxic for us, we did not have the classical examples of work environment discrimination in order to file an official complaint with OIE because we could not point to obvious examples that were in violation of civil rights law or equal employment opportunity. Therefore, the letter we sent to the OIE office did not gain significant traction, and was simply forwarded to the Office of the provost for conflict resolution. In the event that evidence of workplace bullying was proven, it was the responsibility of the provost's office and academic labor relations to follow the AAUP contract for future disciplinary action, and not OIE.

Our Exit Strategy: An Exodus for White Supremacist and Feminist Spaces

By July of 2020, Jennifer, Staci and I had had it! The environment in GWS was so toxic, and so emotionally taxing, that it was literally making us sick. We were full of dread at the idea of having to go back to such an unhealthy and adversarial environment in the fall semester. We felt that the situation was dire and that our very mental and physical wellbeing were at stake. We felt that neither Karen, nor M. Ann and recently, Rachel (another GWS faculty member known for preserving elitist and culturally-biased academic standards for students) had the right to make their colleagues feel this way. It was unfair and we demanded that it stop once and for all! We made it clear that our overall goal was to halt, heal, and mediate the dysfunction and harmful behaviors in our department. In the past three years, we had already gone through all the proper administrative channels (AAUP, CAS Dean's Office, OIE, Mediation, departmental conversations). However, not much seemed to have been done on the part of our institution's management to put an end to the egregious behaviors and the intolerable work climate that we had been forced to endure in GWS during those three years.

In our formal letter of complaint, which we forwarded to OIE and referred to the Provost's Office, Jennifer and I documented everything that occurred in GWS. In addition to wanting our complaints addressed, we also wrote this letter in fear of retaliation and future unprofessional and harmful behaviors from our colleagues, whose behaviors we discussed in the complaint. When our complaint reached the OIE, the OIE director contacted us and told us that she would share with both the President and the Provost what was going on in GWS. By that time, the Provost's Office was already aware of the situation in GWS, as a direct result of the national campaign M. Ann and Karen had launched. I also sent an email to the then provost wherein I requested the transfer of our tenure lines to the Institute of Intercultural and Anthropological Studies (IIAS). This was Staci's suggestion, even though the CAS Dean had previously adopted her own policy that she would not accept tenure-track transfers to that unit. We thus started meetings with the Provost (who was very supportive), a labor relations administrator and the same Dean who previously suggested GWS work the problem out amongst themselves. However, with a new provost the Dean felt pressure to address the issue. Jennifer, Staci, and I informed Bella that we were leaving GWS all together and our Latinx colleague in GWS decided to leave as well.

In October 2020, after a couple of months of ironing out our exit strategy from GWS, Staci, Jennifer, Bella, and I transferred out of the GWS department. Bella moved her tenure completely to another department. Jennifer, Staci, and I moved to IIAS, specifically to teach in the African American and African Studies Program, which was renamed and reinstated from the Africana Studies' previously suspended program. We were given what seemed like a new and safe space to dream about creating new opportunities and work and strive in a stress-free environment—an environment that is conducive to collegiality, respect for one another's humanity, a place of compassion and care for each other (Perryman-Clark et al., 2022). While we have a new environment, we will later discuss how the GWS and Dean's saga continues to affect our lives without much needed accountability from the institution.

The inaction of our institution's administration continued, despite the fact that several administrators and different provosts had been informed about the harm-causing work environment for years. What is the process for remedy to make sure that the conditions that have allowed people who do harm in the workplace are removed? Obviously, just stopping the harm on an individual level is not good enough, though this is precisely what the institution did when it finally allowed Jennifer, Staci and me to move into our new unit, the Institute for Intercultural and Anthropological Studies. Typically, it is the institution that is responsible for establishing processes to prevent a toxic and dysfunctional working environment. It is equally the institution's responsibility to even purport to have specific anti-discrimination and anti-bullying processes in place so that no one has to be the target of harm. However, what if, despite these policies, those who harm do not transform and change? And what if the institution continues to enable these behaviors? If the institution continues to enable these behaviors, restorative justice cannot be achieved.

Unfortunately, restorative justice was also not achieved because we got an apology neither from the dean, nor the institution. And to make matters worse, our colleagues, who caused so much harm to us, have shown neither empathy, nor any sense of accountability for their actions. Furthermore, none of our white feminist colleagues in the department were willing to work out conflict. Therefore, nothing was restored back to its initial state and in the end, there was no healing. As a result of our white colleagues' refusal to acknowledge and be accountable for the harm that they continued to cause, and the administration's inaction despite all our previous complaints, we felt that we had no other choice but to leave the GWS department. We did not understand why the people who have been harmed, most of whom are Black and Brown women, were the ones who had to flee, and therefore becoming fugitives, to a department where our work with feminism could thrive. The lack of institutional accountability to make sure that systemic structure and hierarchies that allow the perpetuation of harm to continue must be fundamentally changed.

What motivates those who harm others to do so with no accountability in such institutions? In which ways do the structures in those institutions allow them to continue to cause harm without showing that they care about those they have harmed? What makes them feel they can shirk accountability even when someone they have harmed or are harming specifically brings it to their attention? What happens when people within an institution intentionally cause harm just to get rid of them? What about power dynamics in the relationships between white feminists and Black women? Why did white feminist colleagues use their Black colleagues to further their own agenda? What about white feminists who do not have any sympathy or empathy? Or those who do not practice the values of feminism? What about those who neither care about, nor value their Black and Brown colleagues or those who neither take responsibility, nor care to change their harmful behavior? According to Michelle Alexander (2012), "racial indifference and blindness- far more than racial hostility- form the sturdy foundation for all caste systems" (p. 242). In other words, it was Karen's and M. Ann's willful indifference to the plight of their Black and Brown colleagues that ensured our subordination, rather than any overtly racist actions that OIE or HR demanded that we prove.

Reinstatement of Africana Studies: Coming Full-Circle to the Institute for Intercultural and Anthropological Studies (IIAS)

Before ending this chapter, it is important to discuss the reinstatement of the Africana Studies Program in relation to the work done by Black women apart from support from white feminists. It is also essential to share this story because it demonstrates how my career has come full-circle, therefore enabling me to do both Black feminist and Diaspora work. When initially established, the Africana Studies Program was designed as a multidisciplinary program that facilitates the study of peoples of African descent around the world with roots in the Civil Rights Movement of the 1960s and 1970s. The aim of programs and departments that teach about the African experience from its inception was to create a more inclusive curriculum in American universities, and to teach African American students about their experiences, histories, struggles, and triumphs in the United States, Africa and in the African Diaspora. After the 1968 student protest, the Black Americana Studies Program was instituted (later named the Africana Studies Program), which ran successfully for over 30 years.

As previously stated, student numbers in the program declined in 2011. Consequently, the program was suspended by the dean's office and M. Ann (who was associate dean at the time) with no attempt from the administration to review or revamp it. In 2013, a group of faculty (myself included) who used to teach in the program, other faculty of color on campus, and a group of concerned administrators, many of whom were Black women, met several times during the summer of 2013 to discuss ways to get the attention of our then CAS dean (a white male) and inform the campus community of the fact that the Africana Studies Program had been "suspended" for the past two years. We insisted that if the institution did not take direct action, the program would quietly disappear. As a group of concerned faculty and staff, I decided to take on the initiative with a group of faculty and lead the process of having the program reinstated.

In the fall of 2014, when that spirit seemed to dwindle, I along with other members of the project team took up where the previous group stopped and were now determined to ensure that the CAS dean's office was well informed about the current situation. We also intended to demonstrate how important AFS still is in higher education. Reinstating the Africana Studies (AFS) Program was based on the concerns of faculty, staff, and students alike for the intellectual harm caused when the administration suspended the Africana Studies Program. The goal of the project was to implement a systemic transformational change towards diversity, equity, and inclusion by advocating, mobilizing and campaigning for the reinstitution of the former Africana Studies Program.

A great irony exists when we consider that an institution of higher education, which prides itself on promoting diversity, inclusion and equity has at the same time 'suspended' and essentially put in the cold storage its AFS program. This action deprived its students of a key multicultural and multidisciplinary academic experience and had sent a mixed signal about the University's acceptance to this field as an important discipline that can contribute as much to students and the campus community as much any other humanities academic area, including, for example, the study of European history and culture and mainstream U.S. history and culture. For these reasons, we planned project events around our aim of bringing together public opinions as a way to help administrators understand the importance and role that an Africana Studies Program plays in the academic experience of all our students in general. We followed through the reinstatement petition by AFS Faculty and designed and conducted workshops and town hall meetings for faculty, staff and students to have their voices heard. Reinstating the AFS was based on the concerns of faculty and students alike, for the harm caused when the administrators suspended AFS.

In the fall of 2015, I personally took the letter with the 500 petition signatures to the dean's office. After all the hard work that the project team and our graduate students put into reinstating the AFS program, several other people, especially past Black and white male Africana studies professors, took credit for our blood, sweat and tears, many of which came from Black women. They acted like they were the ones who were the reason why the AFS program was being reinstated. I personally was not consulted by the dean's office as a potential interim director, despite the fact that I was one of the initiators of the efforts that ultimately led to the reinstatement of the AFS program. I felt that I did not mind the lack of recognition because I didn't do it for fame. I just did it because I believed that it was the right thing to do.

Our Dean (at that time) then appointed a Black man from the School of Social Works as interim director of AFS in 2016 and charged him with revamping the curriculum. Before he stepped down in 2017, the then interim director asked me if I wanted to be director and that he wanted to recommend me to the dean. I told him I was not interested. By that time, I had witnessed so much hypocrisy that I was completely disgusted. I realized that in order to be in a position of leadership, one has to play politics and be in "the old boys' club," so to speak. I wanted no part in that! When the director left in the fall of 2019, an experienced Latinx woman administrator was appointed as the interim director of IIAS, which would house the newly named African American and African Studies Program (AAAS). Primarily the results of my previous labor, AAAS emerged as a revised program that included nine new courses that would count toward the major and our newly vamped "Essential Studies" general education program. After a year, the Latinx director also stepped down, and IIAS was run by an associate dean who served as interim director. It was not until we arrived in IIAS and pointed out this series of unstable interim leadership shifts that we requested a permanent director. With support of the Provost, Staci was nominated to serve in this role.

The point that I also wanted to make in relating this long history of my tenure in the AFS Program is to document the labor that women of color have always done, but which remains unrecognized and undervalued. It is interesting that several men (both Black and white) have built their professional careers in a program that I and other women of color have fought so hard to revive. In the end, we got no recognition for it. That is why it is so important for me to tell this story so that the truth about how the AFS program became the African American and African Studies Program is recorded in the annals of the history of our institution, and how sabotage by white women and white feminists threatened its existence. Now that we have a new unit for the African American Studies Program, where I feel safe from harm under a Black woman feminist director, it is essential for institutions to learn new lessons about the systems they build and the lack of accountability and consequences built for oppressors through such systems.

Concluding Remarks

This chapter is indeed about structures and systems that remain in place, prior to the formation of a Gender and Women's Studies Department that led to much of its demise due to continued toxicity and racial microaggressions. Such toxicity adversely impacted the ability of the Africana Studies Program to thrive, and it took the invisible labor of Black women like myself to save the Africana Studies Program, and eventually flee abuse from the Department of Gender and Women's Studies. It is also critical to discuss how three actors in this narrative, each of whom are both white women and self-identified champions for gender equity, used their power and authority to uphold the system of white supremacy, despite claiming to support all women. Using their power and abuse of power as examples of toxicity, I question how we make sure that the structures that are in place and that allow harm to occur are altered from the root, as opposed to merely shifting personnel from one unit to another. I also insist that we demand accountability from the deans, chairs, and other administrators who are complicit in allowing toxic people to continue to cause harm.

In terms of accountability, this chapter demonstrates how hierarchies of race benefit white women, despite their claims of marginalization. It is interesting to note that the Africana Studies Program was suspended due to personal issues, while GWS has not been held completely accountable. And although the African American and African Studies Program was reinstated in IIAS, it required the labor of Black women to advocate and propose its reinstatement. While I am pleased to come back to where I have started and to continue the work of Black feminists of the diaspora, it is clear that institutions have a lot of work to do with respect to accountability.

· 4 ·

JENNIFER'S STORY
WHITE FEMINIST TERRORISM: BUT I COME WITH RECEIPTS

You are about to learn the biggest Black feminist lesson of your life. Pay attention!

—a Black feminist, former colleague and mentor

Black. Woman. Feminist. Academic. These parts of my identity constantly (and harmfully) propel me toward another set of words—strong, persistent, unbothered, thick-skinned (Gay, 2022), "unfukwitable" (Rodgriguez, 2015), ... I've come to understand that these words are formed in external beliefs and expectations that attempt to forge an inescapable identity of the strong Black woman incapable of experiencing pain.

Rooted deeply within the legacy of the Black Feminisms is an ethos or principles (see Lorde; Moraga & Anzaldua; hooks; Carruthers) of liberation through self-care and self-love. However, within the academy those principles become more realistically a long-suffering path as I juggle and attempt to balance these often competing notions of self: The self-loving, but strong and independent academic; the Black woman who puts her well-being first and rests in her super power of forever being unbothered; and, yes, always reminded, taken to task about, and judged by all that any departure from resilience, strength, and an unnatural ability to bounce back disqualifies me, exposes my ineptitude, halts scholarly productivity, and proves me to be the very imposter that academic institutions always knew me to be.

Frozen in doubt and unable to dream is where I begin, as it is in this state that I attempt to write and right myself out of depression, anxiety, burnout, and feeling trapped; with PTSD—unable to create. In order to express the despair of where I am, and have been for too long, as I write today, it is essential to tell my story, as I know this is a story that many Black women in academia experience (Wagner & Lynn Magnusson, 2005; Anthym & Tuitt, 2019; Haynes et al., 2020). I also join others (Craig & Perryman-Clark, 2011; Perryman-Clark, 2016; Perryman-Clark, 2019; Wallace, 1995) in telling a story that is too often shushed even by the very community that simultaneously claims to love us. That is to say, it is not only white women in the Academy who have bought into white supremacist/feminist ideologies, but also, Black women have internalized the sort of white supremacist/feminist hatred that threatens our very existence in academic spaces. However, as Audre Lorde once said (1985), "I write for those women who do not speak, for those who do not have a voice because they were so terrified, because we are taught to respect fear more than ourselves. We've been taught that silence would save us, but it won't."

What's in Their Name: White Feminist, I Want My Blood Back

"The condition of truth is to allow suffering to speak" (Cornel West, Interview with Charles Blow on *Prime* July 13, 2021).

This story begins in 2015, when I joined a Gender and Women's Studies (GWS) department at an R2 university in a small Midwestern town. It is important to note that I came from (what I thought of as) a progressive and diverse GWS program at an R1 university in a large Midwestern city. As I reflect on my experiences in a predominantly and historically white feminist field, I want to be clear that my work ethos and my research foci are rooted in two central and driving beliefs: (1) healing, like mental decolonization, are life-long projects: my job does not define my life, and my well-being and health should come first. (That said, I also acknowledge that as a Black woman in America, life, all by itself, is full of traumatic events and day to day stressors.) I am also guided by the belief that (2) we teach best what we most need to learn or understand.

Both healing and teaching best what I most need to understand are central to the concept of "bait and switch" in my narrative, as well as others in this book. In this chapter, I attempt to make sense of my experiences in a field and department I naively thought was a safe place to grow in my career, or what I like to refer to as "the bait." As a student, coming from the traditionally white/male-centric field of sociology, where I encountered racism and sexism on a weekly basis, I was completely ready to give up on my decade-long, $250k road to academia. As I finished writing my dissertation, a committee member with a PhD in sociology and professor of Gender and Women's Studies let me in on one of her secrets of success: "you and your work might not find validation within the field of sociology... make new paths toward Black studies and gender studies where you will be more appreciated."

I embraced her advice. For three years in a non-tenure track position, I found peace, joy, and validation amongst women of color colleagues in a large Gender and Women's Studies Department. When I assumed a new role at my current institution, I was shocked to experience the misrepresentation and manipulation—or, "the switch"—that is present in all of our narratives. Later I would learn that my experience would only add yet another perspective and example of Black women's scholarship and presence being co-opted in the academy. Black women's pain, creativity, and work were and continue to be material things co-opted by a department (and University) that claims to stand on the values and principles of diversity, inclusion, and equity. "We want you to come here because your work is great and it makes us look great, but we aren't going to do anything for you and will actually work to make your life miserable, thanks for playing" was the message I (eventually) received loud and clear, but from the place I least expected. Six years later, I am finally processing this trauma and speaking my truth.

In the spring of 2015, after already receiving a job offer that would geographically locate me extremely far away from my father, who was subsequently diagnosed with stage four stomach cancer, I was encouraged by my (then) program chair to apply for a tenure track appointment closer to home; she sent me the following call for applications:

> The Department of Gender and Women's Studies...invites applications for a tenure-track Assistant Professor beginning fall 2015. The position requires a Ph.D. in Gender and Women's Studies or related field, completed or expected by June 2015, as well as experience teaching interdisciplinary Gender and Women's Studies courses. The successful candidate will possess demonstrated potential for teaching and research focused on women and communities of color. Applicants whose work focuses on African Americans are strongly encouraged to apply. The new faculty hire will join six colleagues with full appointments in the Department of Gender and Women's Studies, who typically teach two classes per semester, pursue scholarly research, and contribute to student and program development.

I was excited to not only apply to a place so close to my home town and dying father, but also to a position that seemed so closely aligned with my areas of expertise—one that seemingly placed value on the type of scholarship and teaching that are central to my identity. I sent a letter of application, a portion of which I share here to demonstrate my teaching philosophy, research, and the role my pedagogy played in my interest in the position. It also reflects my alignment with the qualities the department claimed they were looking for:

Dear Department of Gender and Women's Studies Search Committee:

I am writing to apply for the position of Assistant Professor in Gender and Women's Studies... My expertise in intersectional and transnational feminism, Black feminism, sociology, and interdisciplinary methodologies makes me an ideal candidate for this position. My research examines media representations of race, gender, class, and sexuality. In particular, I am interested in the multidimensional ways that Africana women consume, engage, resist, embody, and negotiate popular culture and media images of beauty. Through the use of life story narrative, journaling workshops and healing circles, I bring a unique methodological approach to the study of mainstream media representations and their impact on the lives of Black women.

My pedagogical approach focuses on helping students to understand and articulate their complex social worlds, as well as work on their critical and analytical thinking skills. From constructing a detailed and well-structured syllabus that provides clear schedules and guidelines, to creating a safe environment for open and respectful dialogue, I think carefully about the classroom and its dynamics. The classroom can and should be a space that celebrates and validates individual and group experiences and life narratives. I encourage students to challenge easy or opinion-based assumptions and conventional insights, and I prepare them to encounter topics that might make them feel uncomfortable. In developing a foundation of respect and trust in order to safely navigate the classroom terrain, we engage in a process that looks very similar to the healing circle. We are then able to have respectful disagreements since we learn more from a discussion of many dissenting viewpoints than from a simple consensus.

My pedagogical practices align the importance of feminist praxis, critical thinking, and self-care I strongly believe my combination of critical feminist praxis, work with social media and digital humanities, interdisciplinary research agenda, and commitment to the growth and development of students will continue to make valuable contributions to the department, while enabling me at the same time to engage with scholars and students similarly committed to such issues.

Within ten days I received an invitation to a Skype interview and shortly after a campus job talk. I felt warmly received. In fact, the Chair and her partner (a full professor in the department) led me to feel that my work, and presence was gravely needed in their department. I received an offer faster than any other hiring process I'd previously experienced. I was both relieved and excited.

I floated into this position and through my first year, during what I thought was, for personal reasons, the darkest period of my life. Over the summer of 2015 my father passed away. I received condolences and warmth from my soon-to-be colleagues. My first year flew by as I commuted four hours roundtrip during the first semester, before purchasing a home near the campus. While the first year was a blur, I managed to accomplish some of my writing goals, developed new courses, and started to get my footing in my new environment; I was content to "get by" amongst a small group of women who mostly left me alone. And being left alone, ripe with grief, is what I thought I needed. But by the end of that first year, I looked with hope into the eyes of my new colleagues and said, "Okay, please check on me over the summer. I'm here, single, friendless, and I hope someone will call me for a drink, or something!" When my Chair and I were alone, I reiterated my request and expressed how important it would be to not feel completely isolated and alone. She smiled and wished me a happy summer.

The same Chair would later state, "It is not my job to care about your well-being." In one statement, as she looked through me, my department Chair unveiled the real hell that I stepped into. It was a classic artifice: A tenure-track position that initially had my name written all over it—Black Feminist Scholar—in flashing lights, only for my name to dim towards persona non grata. By the beginning of my second year, everything began to unravel as white feminists began to show their slips. I began my second year, fall 2016, with a voicemail from our institution's Office of Institutional Equity (OIE) instructing me to schedule a meeting with the director of Title IX. As I was making copies of my syllabus and hurrying to prepare for my first day of class, I stopped in to say hello to my Chair, who had not checked on me over the summer. With great concern, I asked her if she knew anything about the OIE situation. She advised me to schedule the meeting and would not offer any further information.

I called OIE and was told that our meeting was needed in order to discuss a complaint that concerned my behavior. In short, when the meeting began, I was given a print out of an email that was sent to the University's central information hub, then to the GWS department assistant, and forwarded to my Chair. The Title IX director, a Black woman, passed me a copy of the email and stated that this was a closed investigation, but brought me there to ask, "Who hates you enough to have written such a vile unfounded complaint?" The email was from a supposed concerned parent saying that her daughter was at a "summer camp" that GWS held, and that while there, her daughter was sexually assaulted "by a professor, Jennifer Richardson—African American—." The Title IX Director was clear that it was from an untraceable email account, and she was aware that no such student was on campus during the summer or at any time (nor was I). Also, GWS did not host any such summer camp or program. So, the Director asked me again, "Who hates you? Do you have any enemies or people here that would want to harm you?"

After wrapping my mind around the situation, I noticed when the email was sent—the day after an ex-partner sent me a text threatening to ruin me professionally. I provided this information to OIE, showing them the text, and was told to work with campus police to make sure he was not allowed on campus. Realizing how unsafe I was all summer, I thought, "Wow! If only my Chair had checked on me this summer. I had no idea I was in potential danger." When I expressed to my Chair these sentiments, adding that as GWS scholars we know all too well how relationship violence can snowball, she dismissed me. She told me that it was not her job to care about my well-being and firmly asserted that she would never call me to check on me or socialize with me outside of work.

By the end of fall 2016, I observed my surroundings with new eyes: the power dynamics that played out as one colleague (Reba) was pushed out of the department and hostilities simultaneously sharpened between my Chair and another colleague (Gloria). I gathered the lesson, like a child in an abusive home: By holding dissenting viewpoints, pushing for fairness and accountability, or questioning the nepotism between the Chair and her partner (let's now call her M. Ann), I embarked on a path that left me in the position of being, not just someone for whom they did not care, but also the enemy. In the final week of the semester, I received a phone call informing me that my mother passed and was instructed that I had to travel two and a half hours back home to claim her body immediately. In shock and panic, the second phone call I made was to my Chair letting her know that I was leaving town and did not know what would happen with my final week of class. She did not offer to cover my classes; she did not inform me that I could take a leave of absence; however, she did advise me to let her know if I'd be back to teach my last two classes. I taught my last week of classes in tears.

Three weeks after my mother passed, over the winter break, I informed my Chair that I was not ready to come back for the start of the spring 2017 semester. Not knowing my AAUP contractual rights, I simply asked that my Chair have someone cover the first four classes (two weeks) as I was not prepared to face students yet. She stalled me by first telling me that she needed to contact HR to see if this was possible. Almost a week later, she told me that she had learned some new information pertaining to HR and that I should reach out to HR to discuss my options. As I tried to gather information on what my leave options were (never thinking to reach out to the union), my Chair began to bombard me with emails and phone calls asking me to give her my syllabi and lecture notes for the time I would be gone. I did not have a syllabus to give her. It was winter break and I was burying my mother and mourning her loss. My Chair's indifference to my mother's death and my cumulative grief was what Cornel West describes as constituting "an intellectual and spiritual bankruptcy of deep depths" (in his 2021 Letter of Resignation to Harvard University).

When I called HR and learned that they were informed by my Chair that I already took a bereavement leave, which was impossible and untrue, I was informed that my only option for paid leave was to take a doctor-approved sick leave. I felt defeated; between HR personnel being unhelpful, at best, and the Chair's heartless calls/voicemails and emails to the tune of:

> ...Of course I'm thinking about this from your perspective and what you need, but I also have to think about the 75 students who are expecting to take their classes with you next semester and expecting to receive the syllabus on the first day of class that explains the expectations and the meetings and everything for the semester. So we need to talk a little bit more about that. But um, we need to get the paperwork going especially if you're requesting sick leave because we'll need some medical documentation for that as well and um with the classes starting in a minute, I want to get this moving quickly..." (Jan 5 2017, 8:55 am—Note that I saved this voicemail on my phone all of these years later)

After running in circles and feeling bullied, I realized that it was taking more energy for me to fight for the benefits to which I was entitled than it would take for me to push out a syllabus and show up to class. I sent an email to my chair, a person who had now shown her bereft ability to ever care about my humanity and well-being:

> I am extremely disappointed in the way that you have treated me and the lack of support during this normal grieving process I am going through. First, you never offered to me any options or support at the time of the death of my mother. You did not mention that I could take funeral or bereavement leave. Second, when I reached out to you via email requesting that you call as soon as possible, you indicated in an email that you did not feel that you could talk to me at all without first talking to HR.

Then you left me a message stating your concerns about what you need to do for the 75 students and their expectations and all of the paperwork that needs to be done in order for a sick leave to take place. When we spoke, you told me that I still needed to talk to HR myself and that you regret leaving that voicemail which I let you know only further stressed me out and made me anxious as I was being asked to consider all the things you need to do for your job in order to be in support of my time off. You told me that you did not know anything about bereavement leave and that because a funeral already took place, I did not qualify for anything but sick leave. When I talked to [Lucy] in HR, she was under the impression, from you, that I already took time off for the funeral and that I did not qualify for any more bereavement leave. I told her that was not true. I did not take time off for my mother's first service. [Lucy] then went on to say that if that is the case, I am entitled to take 5 days for funeral/bereavement leave. I then called you to clarify that my request is that next week I be given bereavement leave. We ended our call with you saying that you still needed to double check and call someone in contracts to make sure that I could really take next week as a bereavement week.

Even though I am feeling unwell, I'd rather withdraw my request for leave and show up for work on Monday and do my best than interact with you or HR or the union regarding this matter. Having to express my needs over and over, having to be told about the strains this puts on you or the concerns you have for how to go about covering my classes, having to be told by [Lucy] in HR that they lost someone and were attending a funeral today because, "Well, it happens," then you telling me that you still have to check whether or not Bereavement leave is something that I qualify for- a very impersonal and belabored process- are all things I do not want to be subjected to. Once again, I am disappointed at the way this department manages individual's well-being and cares for the human needs of our colleagues. As unwell, stressed and depleted as I feel, unfortunately I did not find the compassion and understanding through the process of asking for time off to grieve and recover from the loss of my mother as I had hoped for. Instead, this process has made me more anxious and stressed.

I regret that I did not start this process earlier or know to ask about potential time off that I didn't even know that I would need. However, it is best at this point that I handle my classes to start the semester and if I find that I cannot continue as the semester goes on, I will let you know in as much advance as I can.

To be clear, I will be at work on Monday so any efforts to figure out how to cover my courses in my absence are not required at this time.

She replied:

Hi Jennifer, I take your concerns to heart, and I'm glad you are willing to share them with me. I hope that when you are well we can discuss them further. I understand that you intend to meet with your classes on Monday. I will forward you the clarification message I received this afternoon from [director of academic labor relations] about funeral leave, although it sounds like it's no longer relevant. best...

Afterwards, there was never a real conversation with her pertaining to her harmful behavior. Strangely, she asked to speak to me when I was "well," but had no problem with sending me into the classroom while I was perceived as unwell. Later I would learn from a union grievance officer that, not only was I entitled to bereavement days, but five additional days prior to the start of sick leave.

Midway through the spring 2017 semester—amid increasing hostilities and open arguments between our Chair, M. Ann, and Gloria—the Dean informed my colleagues and me that she was looking for nominations to appoint a new chair. At that time, our Chair was finishing her second three-year term. The department discussed this at a faculty meeting where I asked the Chair directly if she was interested in being nominated as the chair again. She refused to answer. Another colleague, Becca, expressed her interest in being chair. The Chair and her partner, M. Ann, then began to make up rules about the nomination and voting process, despite the Dean's instructions to simply send our nomination to her with a list of strengths and weaknesses for the nominees. Of course, I challenged their woefully contrived process in front of the full faculty. I was ignored by the Chair and M. Ann. The department assistant (at the Chair's direction) reported to the Dean that there were votes for the current Chair (let's now call her Karen), and votes for Becca.

By the end of summer 2017, we would find out that the vote tally was not tabulated correctly, since my nomination was not counted, and since another vote that had been withdrawn and given to Becca, was never taken. When all department colleagues got together, minus Karen and M. Ann, we realized that four of us (Becca, Gloria, Mariam, and I) voted for Becca, leaving one vote (M. Ann's) for Karen. However, prior to the realization that they had falsified the voting results, the Dean reached out and asked various GWS faculty to meet with her to discuss our thoughts about the candidates. Before I could meet with the Dean, I then received an email from Karen accusing me of violating the Family Educational Rights and Privacy Act (FERPA). The retaliation had begun.

I received an email from Karen stating that she was told, by a mystery student, that during my class, I violated FERPA by telling students their grades out loud and in front of the entire class. Of course, that never happened. She instructed me to schedule a meeting with her, but refused to discuss the incident before our meeting. Without ever asking me what actually happened in my class, Karen informed me that she had contacted the Academic Labor Relations Contract Administrator about how she would handle this situation. I immediately scheduled the meeting with her, but I also selected to have a Black full professor ally accompany me at the meeting. This colleague (let's call her Toni) was not only a chair of her own department, but she had a wealth of institutional knowledge, having been there for almost 20 years.

As soon as Karen saw that Toni was with me, her eyes widened. Superseding Karen as the meeting's facilitator, Toni started the meeting. Toni said, "I'm going to talk to you, chair-to-chair: our job is to support our faculty. You heard an account from a student, and instead of telling that student to have a conversation with Dr. Richardson, you not only believed the student without giving Dr. Richardson a chance to respond, but you escalated the situation by contacting the Contract Administrator. If this isn't some type of personal retaliation or punitive vendetta, please explain yourself. But first let's find out what actually happened." Toni then asked me to talk about the events during my class over the past week. I explained that I merely told students that attendance was poor and that, per the syllabus, I would now enforce the three-absence attendance policy. I was then asked by multiple students about how many absences each student already had; so, I told them.

At first Karen tried to defend herself by saying that reading missing attendance numbers was in fact a violation of FERPA. Toni said: "Have you even read the FERPA guidelines? There are some gray areas and it sounds to me like you are looking for anything to pick on Dr. Richardson instead of supporting her." Toni explained how Karen could have and should have handled this situation. Karen began to cry. With a red face full of what some scholars characterize as "white women tears" and victim theatrics (see Cooper, 2018; DiAngelo, 2018), Karen explained that when the student came to her, the student told her that she was afraid to come talk to me (Jennifer). According to Karen, the situation reminded Karen of when she was sexually assaulted in college. She then went on to compare her own experience with sexual assault and being told to confront the person who violated her to this situation and how afraid and helpless my student felt. Yes, she equated her perception of my actions and the impact it supposedly had on my student(s) to her experience of sexual assault as a college student. She made me out to be the angry, criminal Black woman to be feared. In the end, Karen, through weaponized and violent tears, forced a flimsy pseudo apology out of her mouth for not hearing my side first, but ultimately asked me not to discuss attendance with my students again.

By the time I met with the Dean to discuss my thoughts on chair nominations, I shared a very candid and detailed long list of grievances. The Dean listened and shook her head. She responded to each incident with things like, "oh no… I'm so sorry to hear this… this is disturbing… I am definitely going to have to talk to Karen and coach her through these behaviors." In the end, I told her that if Karen were to be reappointed as chair, it would not just mean that I would be uncomfortable in the department, but that the morale of our entire department would suffer. We had already lost two faculty members (Reba and that semester, Gloria) due to Karen and her partner's[1] bullying behavior toward anyone who showed dissent or challenged their ideas. Weeks later, before the new chair was announced, the Dean called me at home. She told me that she needed to talk to me before sending an email to everyone. "If Karen were reappointed," she asked, "would you want to leave the department?" "Yes," I quickly responded, while adding that I'd look for employment elsewhere. She tried to talk me out of my stance by saying that I could report directly to her and bypass Karen; as she then made it clear that she was planning to reappoint Karen. Unfortunately, the Dean never set up her proposed arrangement to have me report to her.

The 2016/2017 academic year ended. Over the summer, my colleagues and I began to bond and build real friendships. We'd been through battle and we were fatigued. We also realized that we had an ally in Staci, a joint appointed GWS faculty colleague, who was not surprised to hear our war stories and was not shy about talking through defense and protection strategies with us. While the greater harm, toxicity, and hostility was still to come, we started to bond in our collective trauma engaged in a sort of pedagogy of sistership—"self-empowerment and self-actualization as a process for solidarity and unity" (McCarthy, 2013, p. 51). When we realized the misinformation regarding the vote, the four of us (including one faculty member, Gloria, who was driven out of the department after M. Ann threatened to call the police if Gloria ever "raised her voice and talked to her like that again" during a faculty meeting) drafted a formal letter to the Dean days before the start of fall 2017 semester:

> It has come to our attention that the result of the GWS chair election was miscounted. We'd like to revisit this and discover where the problem occurred. We must determine moving forward, what the appropriate departmental process should be as the process used in this election was deeply flawed. We wish to inform you that 4

out of 5 faculty voted for [Becca] whereas the election results reported to you and us were 3 votes for [Becca] and 2 for [Karen]. Ultimately, our goal in alerting you to this serious problem is twofold: 1) We want to have the record of this vote accurately set straight; 2) Because the vote reflects other problems in our department, which have many of us feeling that our work environment is becoming increasingly hostile, we are requesting open discussion with all parties—perhaps with a [external mediation service] representative—so that we can move forward in a more collegial environment. We request your prompt attention to this most troubling matter.

We also sent the letter to Karen, M. Ann, and the executive director of OIE. The Dean's response was disheartening. She made clear that her reaction to my feedback and description of a toxic and hostile work environment during our one-on-one meeting was simply performative:

Dear GWS Faculty,

Thank you for alerting me to your concerns regarding the election process for chair of GWS last year. I'd like to reiterate that I do not ask departments to conduct elections for chair, and if they choose to do so, I prefer not to receive numerical count information. My desire, as I expressed last spring, is to receive specific feedback regarding strengths and weaknesses of each nominee. Ultimately, chairs are appointed by administration, rather than elected by faculty. With that said, I take faculty (and staff and student) feedback very seriously in making decisions regarding leadership appointments. Last spring, I did my best to elicit a broad range of feedback, which I considered very carefully prior to making my decision to reappoint [Karen] as chair of GWS. As I stated in the email I previously sent to the department, [Karen] has my full confidence and I look forward to a positive and productive year ahead for the GWS faculty.

I am therefore quite troubled about concerns expressed to me regarding an "increasingly hostile work environment". This is a very serious allegation, and as such, is one that I would like to see followed up on through appropriate channels. These include AAUP, OIE and HR. [We] are also willing to meet with all GWS faculty to discuss our expectations for a collegial, respectful and professional work environment. If you wish to set up a meeting, please do not hesitate to contact [my assistant] to do so.

We reached out to set up such a meeting. We were eventually told by the Dean that she thought it best that we met as faculty and/or in one-on-one meetings with Karen. Through a series of emails we received from Karen, M. Ann, and the Dean, two things were clear: 1) the Dean shared our one-on-one feedback about Karen with Karen, but failed to coach Karen on how to rectify the issues she created, arming her with an arsenal of retaliatory defenses, and

2) Karen was fully in control to deal with us as she and M. Ann saw fit. The Dean washed her hands of us.

In an attempt to make clear the issues that the three of us now faced, we tried to push for mediation. Mariam, Becca and I drafted a letter outlining the issues we wanted to discuss:

> [The Dean] requested that we send individual nominations with feedback to her regarding the appointment of a GWS chair. During a faculty meeting it was discussed that instead of following the Dean's request, we should hold a departmental vote, administered by the dept. Assistant… This was not a unanimous agreement, but at the end of the meeting, it was decided that all faculty would send their nomination to [the assistant] and that the nominations would then be sent to [the Dean]. Votes were counted (inaccurately) and sent to [the Dean]. She again asked for comments and feedback about the nominated faculty (Becca and Karen). During the process of giving feedback (as well as individual/in person meetings) to [the Dean], complaints, problems, and concerns were brought to her attention regarding Karen's role as chair. [The Dean], in individual conversations, acknowledged many issues brought to her attention as problematic or concerning. She made assurances that these issues (particularly if Karen were to be reappointed) would be addressed in some way (e.g., through coaching, having ongoing conversations with Karen, and keeping a close eye on the department). As many concerns were aired about Karen's role as chair, we've yet to address or discuss them in a way that helps us, as a department, to move forward. We are calling a meeting to address this dissonance between the acknowledgment of what many described as a problematic or even hostile work environment and the lack of resolution now that these issues have been voiced and put on the table *and* Karen's reappointment as Chair. As The GWS Department's mission aims to uphold feminist ideals, principles, and values (equality, shared governance, respect, care for one another, an understanding of the correlation between personal and professional lives), many faculty feel that the concerns articulated to [the Dean] are not reflective of the reality of how this department operates as a whole and are not aligned with our feminist principles. We would like to discuss the following:
>
> 1. The voting process and outcome as it pertains to how business is done in this department:
>
>   o The scare tactics involved in telling us not to send individual nominations to the Dean despite her request
>   o The inaccuracy of the vote
>   o The perception of wrongdoing and climate of distrust
>   o [dept assistant] told Mariam that Jennifer did not vote which was inaccurate/inappropriate… While it is completely the right of the Dean to appoint whomever she desired, what was the point of soliciting feedback? The impact of this stirred the pot of shared concerns and

unpleasant work environment but left faculty with no resolution or comfort.
- The effect of exposing all of our concerns about Karen's leadership, then reappointing her makes for an even more uncomfortable and distrustful working environment

2. Lack of transparency, openness, and shared governance (leads to distrust amongst other things)

- Unresponsive to faculty concerns ("if you don't like [it], file a grievance")
- Sharing the position of chair/supporting and encouraging colleagues who express interest
- Silence and secrecy ("did you tell others about your dissatisfaction with the way I treated your request for support of your adoption process?")
- Cherry picking and asking for input on certain things like belaboring the details of [Rachel's], (a newly transferred faculty member with a track record of discord in another department) terms of joining our dept but not discussing [Reba's], (who left the department) terms to stay in our dept
- Discussing and having input on important issues that impact all of us (e.g. [Reba] and [Gloria] leaving)
- Discussing areas of conflict (and how things should be/or are handled) as a whole instead of siloes or secret one on one conversations; or shutting dissent and disagreement down completely (labeling people as trouble makers- who is next?)
- Why did the AAUP write a letter of support for Karen? Who solicited this letter? How did the union get involved?

3. Lack of concern about faculty well-being and lack of advocacy for faculty concerns (both personal and professional)

- Not giving faculty preference over part time or grad students
- Setting a climate where actions are aligned to the declaration that "it is not," Karen's "job to care about [faculty] well being."
- Listening to student complaints about faculty violating FERPA and contacting Contract Administrator before actually talking to the faculty to find out what happened
- Not supporting faculty during personal time of need as human beings and instead, sticking to the "letter of the law" or being cold and distant (e.g. instead of checking on a colleague's well being, telling them that

it is not your job to care, not supporting a colleague that is struggling to start a family because "legal" said that the Chair cannot do this, telling a colleague that you will not send her application for funding to CAS because it is poorly written and will make us look bad, not telling a colleague about bereavement leave after the death of *another* parent and then making taking sick leave more burdensome and difficult, listening to a student complaint without asking the student to talk to the instructor, contacting faculty about student allegations late on a Friday and not being available to communicate further)

4. Retaliatory behaviors and the shutting down of dissent

o Karen and M. Ann's treatment of Gloria during a faculty meeting; shutting her up when Gloria wanted to tell everyone else how Karen unfairly treated her in her attempt to apply for CAS funds
o Karen and M. Ann threatening to call the police on Gloria because she raised her voice during a faculty meeting
o Mariam received a scolding email from M. Ann advising her not to push for an outside chair
o Everyone receiving an email from M. Ann and not responding due to the hostile, defensive, and scolding tone
o Soon after the votes were made public, based on what appears to be a retaliatory environment, it seemed that Karen's treatment of Jennifer pertaining to the accusation/concern of violating FERPA was deemed retaliatory

5. Fellow faculty leaving the department and others desiring to leave due to the current/previous environment

o Does it concern administration as to why this is happening?
o Can we have an honest conversation about what this means moving forward?

6. Resolutions toward a departmental cultural shift including discussing what we'd like shared governance and transparency to look like, and evidence that our Chair hears and responds to our concerns

o What can shared governance look like? What is possible? What is Karen willing to do?

- o Evidence that Karen is hearing these concerns: lack of trust; receiving feedback; humility; control and power dynamic (especially as it pertains to M. Ann); advocating for faculty and acknowledging that our personal lives do affect our professional lives.
- o Could a departmental cultural shift take place or is it too late? What happens if 1–2 more people leave (as they are considering) and does administration care?

Ultimately, through a variety of oppressive tactics, Karen and the Dean made it so that this conversation never materialized into anything fruitful. Karen wasted two months of our time going over some "civility" etiquette for rules of faculty meeting interactions, as if we were in kindergarten. She also imposed on us the presence of the "Advisory board" members, even after we requested that some of our departmental meetings be just with the core GWS faculty. She did not care about our requests. She completely dismissed and ignored them. M. Ann went to the extent of wanting to police even our nonverbal communication, demanding, for example, that we should neither acquiesce or shake our heads in disapproval. Neither were we to show facial expressions of disagreement in response to what a colleague said during our meetings. We were bullied into submission and spent the next year under surveillance, constantly looking over our shoulders.

In fall of 2017, I attempted to transfer to another department, as I had forewarned the Dean. Reportedly, Karen had already poisoned the well there, telling colleagues in the new department that I was the "troublemaker" and that it was "Jennifer pulling and instigating Mariam and Becca." I learned as much from a colleague (Lauren, who actually showed me an email between her and Karen) who worked in the intended transfer department. Learning this also helped make sense of the moment that a faculty member in that department physically fled from me as she ran down the hallway. I was simply trying to schedule a meeting with her and she sprinted away from me like I was a monster in a horror movie. I eventually withdrew my transfer request. At one point, M. Ann attempted to pull Becca to her side of things (according to Becca) by telling her something to the effect of "Jennifer has been through so much, personally, can you really trust her account of anything?"

Not only was I deemed the antagonist and instigator, but now I was too crazy to be a reliable narrator of my own experiences. Angry. Black woman. Liar. From my graduate students being told, by Karen and others, not to put me on their committees, to Karen harassing me into attending a workshop on microaggressions, the list of my grievances was long. I felt hurt, humiliated, and exhausted. They'd taken too much of my blood with their "witchcraft" (or an expanding trend in feminist literature where white women appropriate Black Diasporic magic in the pursuit of power, which likely explains the alleged story of one of our GWS colleagues literally attempting to carry vials of African peoples' blood home with her from her travels to The Continent). I consulted with the AAUP, other colleagues, and the then interim Provost (a white woman ally) at the time. They each validated my grievances as both legitimate and actionable. Regrettably, many incidents had already passed the timeframe in which I should have filed grievances. Close to the end of the 2017/2018 academic year, I eventually succumbed under the constant barrage of their harm and terror. With the volunteer assistance of the interim Provost, I was able to bypass Karen and take a long overdue medical leave of absence. By then, I was deeply estranged from my scholarly writing, suffering severe depression and anxiety, engulfed in rage, and exhausted in the mere number of hours given to this battle for justice. And of course, like so many women of color faculty, (Smith, Vidler, & Moses, 2022; Cox, 2008; Torres, 2020) I had to request a pause to my tenure clock.

By the 2018/2019 academic year, things seemed to calm down for me. Rachel, a new addition to our department, transferred in with my initial support and the support of Becca and Mariam, despite the shade and doubt cast on Rachel by Karen and M. Ann. Also, with a new Provost on board (whom Staci discusses in her narrative) and a university-wide curriculum overhaul, Karen and M. Ann seemed less interested in power hoarding and instead presented the guise of shared governance, as each of us were responsible for doing our part in revamping courses. This new chill out time probably came after Karen drew negative attention from upper administration and the union grievance officers for her behavior toward Mariam before the fall 2018 semester began. As she'd done with me, Karen bullied and harassed Mariam about her request for medical leave. However, this time, her behavior was eventually chastised by the AAUP union grievance officer, and Mariam was able to take her leave. Mariam tells this story in the previous chapter. Needless to say, trust was still broken, and the politics of our interactions were clear: Karen and M. Ann were hostile toward the new Provost for reasons Mariam, Staci, and I were oblivious about; the Dean was taking inventory of our department with the threat of raising teaching loads for unproductive faculty, even though she'd recently given us a new faculty line; and the truth of past harmful behaviors of Karen and M. Ann had become well known within the University.

In no way were we in the clear. Another factor that helped us merely survive, if only to achieve departmental objectives that academic year, was that M. Ann was on sabbatical. After her sabbatical, she was not frequently on campus, as she had the luxury of teaching primarily online, reflecting just one of many examples of the rampant nepotism within our department. By the end of the spring 2019 semester, through thinly veiled hostilities, we were able to hire another woman of color. Looking forward to another ally in our new hire [Bella], and with strengthened bonds of Staci, Becca and Mariam, I was hopeful about the 2019/2020 academic year. It would also be Karen's last year as chair.

With that, at the beginning of fall 2019, Karen feigned a bright smile and attempted to make personal connections. Reportedly, she even invited Bella to meet up over the summer for a bike ride. Karen's attempt at pleasant small talk and token sharing was laughable, but definitely not unnoticed or unappreciated. Her white lady niceness was fake, transactional, and yet still a relief from the nastiness of the past.

There were brief moments during fall of 2019 that I was able to breathe. Despite the red flags and warnings: "The women's movement enlists the support of Black women only to lend credibility to an essentially middle-class, irrelevant movement... Time has shown that there was more truth to these claims than their shrillness indicated," (Wallace in Guy-Sheftall, 1995, p. 225) I foolishly began to dream about finally catching up on all of the writing projects that fell in the cracks of the past three years. I ended that semester and winter break with renewed hope but noticed the severe loss of energy, time, tears, and blood. I wanted it all back.

Turning the Corner: Reimagining Healing

I operate from a particular ethos in my Black Feminist praxis: self-care and self-love are crucial to all work that I do (the work of life and profession). I left the field of sociology because any work birthed out of this ethos was not valued by my peers and mentors at that time. Perlow et al. (2018) contend that for Black women, particularly in the academy, "[d]espite numerous academic and political accomplishments, so many Black women carry a *brave bruised girlchild* inside of them. She has continually been told that she is not good enough, not smart enough, and that she does not deserve to let her light shine. Even though Black women are often able to intellectualize our awareness of the negative socio-political messages constructed about us, it is not easy to escape their impact" (p. 7). Contending with harm means finding multiple paths toward healing; and rerouting those paths constantly.

In much of my work, I contend that "[i]n order to produce true social transformation and strive for a radical notion of collective freedom, we must pay attention not only to our political/ideological positions, but also to our individual and collective practices of self-care and healing—practices that are themselves deeply political" (Richardson, 2018, p. 282). Focusing on defining the potential and process of healing, especially in the DEI work of research, service and teaching has been my intellectual pursuit. While Black feminist tradition has historically included radical self-care and well-being (see the work of Toni Cade-Bambara, Audre Lorde, Barbra Smith, and June Jordan to name a few), too much has been lost in our praxis. However, I've found that excavations of healing as a political path of resistance challenges the traditional boundaries of the academy. Once more, we teach best what we most need to learn; and I believe that my particular Black feminist ethos is what interested or inevitably brought Keiondra and Olivia to me as graduate students (as I subsequently discuss). In "Healing Circles as Black Feminist Pedagogical Interventions" (2018, p. 284), I've argued that:

> [H]ealing is an act of resistance to oppression that can produce counter knowledge, celebrate the spirit, and foster community through affirmation and sharing, particularly as it pertains to Africana women. When I invoke the term "healing," I seek a continuation of Audre Lorde's (1976, 1984) work, which locates healing at the center of our interactions not just with ourselves, but also with our students, co-investigators/subjects, colleagues, and others. Merging insights from hooks (1994, 2005), Leary (2005), Collins (1998), Lorde (1976, 1984), and Ani (2000) [...] I weave together a particular definition and description of healing that includes the following overlapping goals and stages: (1) decolonizing the mind, by "breaking with the ways our reality is defined and shaped by the dominant culture and asserting our understanding of that reality, of our own experiences" (hooks, 2005, p. xxxii); (2) finding and maintaining spaces of joy and affirmation—or reclaiming the living room spaces and safe places in our lives (Jordan, 1985); (3) becoming less concerned with affluence and materialism (Collins, 1998; hooks, 1981, 2003) and instead focusing on self- determination and the reclamation of non-essentialized identities (e.g. cultural/ ethnic or sexual identities), spaces, spirituality, knowledge, community, and lineage; and (4) recognizing and fostering critical awareness of a political path of resistance toward self-recovery and wholeness (Richardson-Stovall, 2012).

It is in these erotic spaces within ourselves, and in communion with others, that this wounded healing (Hill, 2009) can utilize our collective knowledges as validation, learning resources of coping and therapeutic mechanisms. From these spaces new visions of anti-racist feminist liberation and futures become possible. Knowing this from a point of research methodology and pedagogy, trauma and crises still has a way of creating silos, panic, and painful stagnation. This work, in and of itself, to heal is not only a lifelong pursuit, but can be more challenging than any other professional or personal endeavor. Years of abuse in GWS certainly have taught me as much.

Here it is so important to discuss the significant roles that both Keiondra and Olivia played in my journey—in my story of survival and healing. In Chapter 6, both Olivia and Keiondra share more in depth about our relationships and incidents that occurred when they were graduate students. My relationship with these two students, starting in the fall semester of 2016, is not only valued because of the allyship, mutual support, and friendship that evolved over the years; my time with Olivia and Keiondra changed and elevated who I am as an educator and advocate for my students. They were deeply committed to filling the gaps that their graduate program left with their knowledge of Black feminist thought. Our connection involved more than just our incredible intellectual work; the three of us also connect over losing a parent during the same timeframe. Furthermore, we didn't just talk Black feminist theory; we practiced it in our care and respect for one another. At times Keiondra and Olivia were more concerned with what they could do to support me, check in on me, and care for me, than anything they needed from me as their mentor or committee member.

Over the past decade of teaching in higher education, I've come across only a handful of students like Olivia and Keiondra, whose work ethic, breadth of intelligence, and loyalty to Black feminist ethos are truly authentic and palpable with all they engage. When talking about our book with other Black women in higher education, one colleague asked why we chose to give so much space in this book to Olivia in particular (as a white woman) and to Keiondra (as a former student who was not a part of faculty in GWS). For me, there are multiple answers and reasons for our choices pertaining to their contributions here. However, the simplest and most compelling reason is that they were in fact, in action, in the day to day-ness of the fight for Black women surviving white feminist spaces. They were our witnesses, they were our defenders, and they did not simply leave with their degrees and wish us luck. They stayed in the arena with us as co-conspirators; and they carried Black feminist lessons with them in their own political, academic, and activist work. While I consider them my contemporaries or peers, ultimately, Olivia and Keiondra will carry Black feminist lessons, truths and possibilities for longer than we can. And I cannot overstate how much I trust in their capacity, willingness, and skill to do just that.

With my sister/allies clinging together, I came into spring 2020 ready to nominate and provide feedback to the Dean for a new chair. However, January 2020 started first with an epidemic of white women vying for power. Every single white person in GWS put their hat in the ring to become chair, including Rachel, (who forced her transfer from trial to full transfer, despite Mariam, Becca, and my protest), and a joint appointment faculty, male colleague. It was clear that they formed a coalition against Becca becoming chair. It was like watching vultures fight over prey. White feminists, one by one, each stood up to explain why they did not want to be chair but were willing to become chair because "no one was more capable than they were." Rachel, Karen, and M. Ann each said they did not want the chair position to fall to an incompetent or outside of the department faculty member. Becca, to whom they each were indirectly and passively referring, was the only person who stood up and discussed why she really wanted to become chair. She also outlined the visions she had of a better, more collaborative department. I wish that I could report that Becca was the best choice. Instead, in her singularly-focused obsession to become chair, and to prove her self-worth and belonging, she really became the lesser, or more well known, evil. The friendly dynamic between the three of us (Mariam and I on one side and Becca) or our "cabal," as we were characterized behind our backs, was starting to crack.

A couple of months into spring 2020, I was really ready for the infighting and reinvigorated hostilities to be over. We received surveys from the Dean, the same dean who previously reappointed Karen. This time, the Dean attempted to collect our thoughts on each candidate in a much more structured and anonymous survey. Clearly, she learned from the past chair appointment fiasco. We put the election speeches and survey behind us and moved on with both weariness and extreme distrust, albeit with the hope that the ship could still be righted and recovered under Becca's leadership. And then the reality of COVID-19 hit. Like many, we scurried to adjust, to put classes online, to stay home and not panic, and in many ways were siloed, as there was no sense of collegiality or community university-wide. Mariam, Becca, Bella, Staci, and I tried to stay connected and sane as we chatted and helped each other through the transition. However, just as we were taking another deep gasp for "sanity now!!!" the Dean, along with the rest of upper administration (and much of what many experienced in higher education), began talks of pay cuts, job cuts, higher teaching loads, and the possibility of not appointing a chair to our department at all.

In Chapter 3, Mariam goes into depth about the events of the summer of 2020 that eventually led to every single woman of color faculty (including Bella and our joint appointed colleague, Staci) leaving the GWS department. As painful as it has been to look back at hundreds of email exchanges, it has been a useful exercise. The collecting of grounding artifacts not only displays the insidious tension and hostility within our department, but most interestingly illustrated the foreshadowing of and fear pertaining to the idea that if Karen and M. Ann did not heal the dysfunction, more faculty would leave our small department. This sentiment was put forth, primarily by Becca, in multiple interactions over the years. At first, she aligned her interests in allyship with me and Mariam because she also questioned and pushed back on Karen and M. Ann's bullying over power in GWS, though she had a reputation of aggression and toxicity, as labeled by her former department. While we initially bonded, during the pandemic her motives would become clear that she wanted to serve as chair for a salary increase and courted our support for that primary reason. After learning more about her (especially her political stance during the 2020 summer of Black murders), it became quite clear that she was always more concerned with the possible dismantling of the entire department and the future of GWS than focusing on how individuals' behaviors were harmfully impacting lives. She wanted to maintain the department to initially protect her chair's salary, and she knew that her reputation would limit her ability to transfer to a different department beyond GWS. Nevertheless, Becca was, if nothing else, correct in worrying about the departure of additional colleagues and the possible obliteration of that white feminist haven (more on the current state of GWS in Chapter 7).

Much of the following comes from a 170-page document that Mariam and I wrote as a formal complaint to OIE and ultimately the Provost and President in 2020. This 170-page letter, along with Bella's formal complaint and Staci's conversations with administration, were the impetus to our eventual exodus from GWS to another department:

> The dysfunction, stressful and hostile work environment, and the endless drama in GWS that started years ago, is just getting worse and worse by the day. The situation is getting more and more unbearable, despite the fact that we are supposed to be on summer vacation, and despite the fact that Mariam Konaté had shared on two occasions in emails to the entire faculty in early June that their emails are heightening our anxieties, and despite the fact that Bella shared that the situation has led to her

to a mental health issue and that she is seeking professional help. We definitely think the environment is so toxic, and so emotionally taxing, that it is literally making us sick and we are dreadful at the idea of having to go back to such an unhealthy and adversarial environment in the fall semester. We have already gone through all the proper administrative channels (AAUP, CAS Dean's Office, OIE, Mediation, departmental conversation) within the past three years. However, not much seems to have been done on the part of … Management to put an end to the egregious behaviors, and unacceptable work climate that some of us have been forced to unfairly endure in GWS for years now. We think that neither Karen, nor M. Ann (and recently, Rachel) have the right to make the rest of us, their colleagues, feel this way. It is unfair and not right, and we demand that it stops once and for all!

To be clear, our overall goal is to stop/heal/mediate the dysfunction and harmful behaviors in our department, and these are the three reasons this demand is predicated on:

1. This has a long history; but our story will start with the toxic culture that Karen and M. Ann have created prior to the Dean's mismanagement in reappointing Karen as chair; and the fall out after she was reappointed.
2. Then we want to point out and discuss the spike in dysfunction and hostile environment when the latest chair nomination process started; how recent racial unrest and issues concerning faculty of colors' well-being was handled by both Karen as chair as well as our non POC colleagues.
3. Which all leads to the destruction and mismanagement that is currently happening under Becca's chairship. While she made some wrong moves directly before becoming chair, the toxic and hostile culture of the department and deplorable behavior of Karen, M. Ann, and Rachel needs to be addressed, as it is having a direct impact on how Becca, our new Chair, is able to do her job.

Although we had already made both the CAS Dean, OIE and the AAUP aware of the issues that have been going on in GWS dating back to August 2017 and April 2018 respectively, ultimately, we would still like to see OIE, the AAUP, and the Provost's Office involved. We want to document everything that has been going on in GWS for fear of retaliation and future unprofessional and harmful behaviors from our colleagues whose behaviors we are discussing in this complaint. Nevertheless, we'd love to see everyone (together or individually) called to the table so that we could achieve a satisfactory resolution and restore a climate in GWS that we all feel safe and valued to work in. Unfortunately, our past formal complaints and informal conversations with individuals from administration and the AAUP have yielded no improvements nor action steps.

In all of this twisting and turning, pleading for our humanity and our ability to focus on our scholarly work, the constant cycle of harm, wounds, healing (rinse and repeat) was devastating. But finally, we were freed from GWS

with the hands-on assistance of the Provost who was our advocate, even going above the Dean to make sure we were all supported. Unfortunately, the Provost suddenly stepped down from her position, only weeks before my tenure file was set to be forwarded to the Provost for review. Also, days before the fall 2020 semester began, Becca would be appointed chair and GWS would stay intact; Karen and M. Ann's dooms day did not occur but they immediately began retaliating against Becca as chair. But that was for them to figure out as Mariam, Staci, and I were free from that space and no-contact orders for every remaining member of GWS went into effect. I have not heard from or seen GWS faculty since then and I must admit, in many ways, that has been glorious. At this point in time, new understandings and possibilities of my healing journey were coming into focus.

My ethos of *heal thyself first* is evermore intact, especially after in-depth therapy, and medication. Having a committed sisterhood with my now three other Black colleagues in our new department, we have finally begun to reclaim our power and humanity. (An additional Black woman colleague from another college transferred a joint appointment to our new home in IIAS.) We cry together. We feed each other. We celebrate our Blackness and our magic. We root for each other. We laugh with each other sometimes until our sides hurt. We are still in treacherous territories that systemically threaten to continue the harm; however, we are just not alone in the dark.

Conclusion: Wholeness and Truthtelling

Much of what we write in these chapters, our stories, are incomplete indictments; each of us could write hundreds of pages with evidence documenting the vials of blood that these white women snatched from our bodies, figuratively and literally; we could each provide countless pages of historical and theoretical analysis of a story that is all too common for most Black women in the academy. But there is always power in unearthing the dead, the silenced, and unleashing our truths. And we continue to create, dream, and find places of joy and community even as we struggle and find ways to live and wrestle with questions and considerations. As I collect the bruised pieces of myself, pushing myself to dare to imagine and create, it is through telling my truth and airing things out that I can move onward.

I also continue to explore questions to which there are no clear or easy answers: How do we recover ourselves, heal, and move forward once we've escaped the hostility and toxicity, especially if we still live and work within an institution that allowed such harm in the first place and did not hold perpetrators accountable? As new politicized conversations emerge regarding racism as a public health crisis, solutions in both recognizing systemic racism and the work to repair targeted populations must be done (Feagin & Bennefield, 2014; Tipirneni, 2021). But by whom? Alas, these problems are as old as this country. And simultaneously efforts to attack Critical Race Theory (CRT) and the historical truths of racism and patriarchy are well underway. As Nikole Hannah-Jones' recent move to Howard University demonstrates, it is not the job of Black women alone to endure harm, remain within anti-Black spaces, AND heal ourselves within those spaces merely on the strength of promises of change, or "the bait." Not only are we expected to heal our wounds and get over it, we are also expected to create pathways, maps, treatises, prescriptions and all the answers for our abusers in order for them to get ready to maybe stop abusing us.

The repetitive telling of a troublesome tale is not an indictment of the tellers; rather it is informative to survivors that our plight is not imagined nor happening in isolated sets of actions. However, I do not believe we reach true liberation merely in our telling, as often the retelling goes beyond compiling evidence, data, and proof, toward the building of totems. White women's labors of harm under the guise of feminism is not a new trend of behaviors. These systemic attacks on women of color in the academy are calculated and designed to uphold patriarchy and white supremacy; especially in white feminist spaces—the places we assume are (or believe should have been) most safe and sacred. "Black women scholars must maintain a constantly militant and critical stance toward the places where we must do our work. We must also begin to devise ways to break down our terrible isolation in the white-male academy and to form the kinds of support networks Black women have always formed to help each other survive" (Hull et al., 1982, p. 22). And still, this type of vigilance can be exhausting in and of itself.

I wish that I could end my story with a neat and pretty bow. But I am in the book of *Revelations* so to speak—the battle continues as I simultaneously write an appeal for my tenure and promotion file (only to be denied and then go up for early tenure again six months later). Yes, I love working with Mariam and Staci in what feels for the moment like a safe haven or foster home; however, AAAS is not my academic home. In addition to relocating from my academic home, I also believe that there was no tangible institutional accountability on the part of the abusers, pointing most importantly to administrators like our dean and interim provost (white and male). I cannot offer closure to my story while I am still experiencing severe PTSD. I suffer and struggle everyday through depression and anxiety to teach, to attend meetings, and to be scholarly or productive. I've been simultaneously juggling: looking over my shoulder and for the sky to fall; being told to get over it and be happy with where I am now; attempting to write, and teach; and heal.

Healing then becomes an exercise that is done in community with my battered and unrecognizable self (a version of me that is built on past traumas) and my amazing sisters who have risen above and beyond to have my back. Healing happens when I remember that struggle will always be present as this place was not made for our survival or humanity. While AAAS is not my "home" department, but a refuge space, it is beginning to feel more and more like home. Similarly, I feel more whole every day. And I am grateful to know that I am seen in our collective; as we "share the strengths of each other's vision as well as the weaponries born of particular experience" (Lorde, 1991, pp. 68–69).

Notes

1 While we do not advocate for identifying women's relationship statuses as integral to their professional careers, it is important to emphasize Karen's partner here because both believed that either one of them should be department chair to maintain their power over the department. The nepotism and use of two headed chair antics strengthened their positions and was a constant point of contention within the department as it frequently came up in faculty meetings.

· 5 ·

STACI'S STORY
RACISM, GENDER AND ADMINISTRATION: THE PERILS OF HEALING IN HIGHER EDUCATION'S PUBLIC EYE

Like the previous two chapters, this chapter also is a story of Black women's trauma in white and feminist spaces, spaces where feminism could not save me. While Mariam and Jennifer were experiencing trauma under the auspices of whiteness and white supremacy in GWS, I was also experiencing traumas of white supremacy from many–if not all sides, including white men and Black women. In Jennifer's chapter, she stated, "it is not only white women in the Academy who have bought into white supremacist/feminist ideologies." This statement rings also true with my story when I served as associate dean of an honors college, where I was also the only woman and African American in the college's leadership. I was also one of two faculty in the college, with the other being the white male dean. The men in this narrative claimed to be supportive of women's issues, with one being a licensed family therapist who specialized in queer and transgender therapies, and the other claimed to conduct workshops on overcoming toxic masculinity. And, Black women in this narrative claimed to be as "woke" and progressive as they come, but none of these folks could save me from misogynoir; in fact, each contributed to it.

The purpose of sharing trauma from two different units highlights the experiences of Black women in the academy as ones not limited to one academic department; rather, these experiences are characteristic of institutional cultures. I was isolated from other Black women faculty, including Jennifer and Mariam, since I was the only Black woman administrator in the unit. Like Jennifer and Mariam, I also lacked support from Black and feminist allies in the academy. Although I tried to keep in contact with both Jennifer and Mariam during my tenure in administration, overall, I suffered extreme isolation, due in great part to the existing academic silos in higher education. This story draws from the lens of Afrofuturism to reimagine a new home for collaboration with Black women and healing. But the story and pain begin like this:

This Is a Story of Trauma: A Story of Healing: And a Story of a Future: The Beginning

Imagine being stunned that staff, including several women and Black women, have expressed numerous complaints about your leadership and have accused you of making racialized and inappropriate comments that made even Black women feel uncomfortable. Imagine being accused of undermining leadership and dismissing staff concerns without any context for these allegations. Imagine having no knowledge or specifics about any allegations or complaints that currently exist against you and feeling the need to resign from your position due to staffing pressures. Imagine experiencing all of this while continuing to leverage your position as both a tenured professor and administrator to serve as an ally for those untenured, bullied, and unable to speak for themselves. Imagine having to defend yourself against white men and women at the same time.

This is precisely what happened to me, as a result of experiences that mirrored Jennifer's, as she reveals in the previous chapter. By 2019, I had completed the very first year of my first dean's level administrative assignment of a three-year contract in the Honors College that could be described as anything but typical. The environment historically has been seen as one lacking racial diversity, although my hire was designed to improve racial diversity. Like Jennifer, these folks also would feign an excitement over my hire that would soon fade. In fact, after asking BIPOC students why they would not join the Honors College even though they met the academic requirements, the refrain I heard over and over is that it is not a place for people of color, especially African Americans. I learned they were right.

Promotion, Lack of Onboarding and Toxic Work Environments: Throwing Black Women into the Deep End

In 2018, was promoted to associate dean of the college. My appointment was for three years, but I served my first year without a formal review by my dean. On the second day of my appointment, the dean, notably a white cis-heteronormative male whose research focused on queer and transgender family therapy, decided to take a two-week vacation. When I asked what work I should do in his absence, I was told to meet with 9 staff members and read an 18-page handbook. That's it. No formal onboarding. Throughout the coming months I quickly learned that my first administrative appointment would rely on me training myself and at times managing up, a practice shared in countless narratives of Black women in higher education (Garrett et al., 2022; West, 2022; Gonzalez, 2021; Garrett & Thurman, 2018). While many of these narratives may differ in specific details, they each have a similar refrain: BIPOC women must fend for ourselves when being promoted to new positions in the workplace and higher education; and like Jennifer's story shows, no one is about to check on us or care about our wellbeing.

After meeting with staff during the dean's vacation, each expressed multiple concerns about the dean's leadership. They also blamed the dean and various other staff for the toxic culture of the unit and practices as I was told by multiple staff members that spanned a couple years and included the dean's repeated offenses of making inappropriate and sexist comments against women and BIPOC students, some of which I would later experience personally. A couple staff members disclosed another white female colleague's personal blog offering, on several occasions, ramblings, and personal attacks against other staff in the college. My then eight-year old child and I also emerged as targets of her ramblings, many of which were quite racist. For example, on the same day I went to recruit Black students from a predominantly Black high school in Detroit, an event she initially was tasked to schedule, before insisting that the school had yet to respond). She published a blog advocating that the U.S. give Detroit to Canada because of its uselessness. In other posts, she would praise Andrew Jackson, the former president most famous for indigenous genocide. This same staff member would later cry white woman tears after sharing the ways the current position had negatively impacted her health.

Despite learning about some of the staff's toxic behaviors, I tried to listen carefully. I asked each staff member to identify ways I might help them do their jobs better. Several made recommendations that I not be afraid to express concerns about the office climate and microaggressions, since they claimed the dean had previously made racial and gender-based comments that were microaggressive. They expressed confidently that if he would listen to anyone who speaks their mind, it would be me. They (and previous staff including the retired white woman administrator whom I would replace) expressed their regrets for not speaking up and taking a stand. They wished they possessed a similar courage, but were pleased that I did. They encouraged me to express my courage and emphasized with confidence that there would be no negative consequences. One staff member even expressed, "you're a woman of color in leadership. They know not to mess with you." The recommendation I'd take from them would end up leading to my eventual termination from the unit.

Leaves of Absence: Black Women as Mammy and Caretakers of White Work

Two months into my new role, the dean took an extended leave of absence. An absence that was intended to last two weeks ended up lasting seven months. During most of the entire first semester of my new leadership, I was required to serve simultaneously as a de facto dean sans official appointment and associate dean. When I asked the current dean about his comfort level with me making operational decisions in his absence, I was initially told to run decisions by the academic advising director, another white, cis-heteronormative male who lacked a terminal degree or faculty rank, in the unit. (The advising director also studied with Keiondra under the doctoral program, but later withdrew from the program completely) It wasn't until the end of the semester that I had the courage to ask the provost for additional compensation for doing two jobs, to which the then provost agreed was earned and warranted. For my efforts, I received an additional stipend from October through December, which was for more months than I expected.

While required to run every decision by a white male academic advisor who was known for conducting workshops on toxic masculinity, I was still held responsible for taking care of the unit and fulfilling the responsibilities of a dean without the recognition of my adopted position. This behavior aligns closely with the historical roles of Black women as mammies. As Cheryl Johnson (1994) describes of bell hooks' work,

Many black women, she argues, are constructed into the mammy role, "nurturing and sustaining the life of others" (154). She states further that "Black women in all walks of life… complain that colleagues, co-workers, supervisors, etc. ask them to assume multi- purpose caretaker roles, to be their guidance counselors, nannies, therapists, priests" (154). (p. 413)

This is precisely what the dean and perhaps administration expected me to do: Assume a wide range of roles without offering any support, acknowledgment, compensation, or respect—that is, until I requested it.

More recently, Ronisha Browdy (2017) explores the concept of mammy as related to forced labor where Black women were forced into Southern slave owners' homes as "midwives, nurses, cooks, confidants" (p. 403), and wet nurses (West & Night, 2017) as a co-opted myth. This false caricature often forms into stereotypes including the "strong Black woman" and other characterizations that present Black women as the aggressive or angry woman on one hand, and the Black Matriarch or Mammy, as a quintessential nurturer and caregiver on the other hand. Ultimately oppressors used these stereotypes to dehumanize Black women and justify physical abuse and the sexual exploitation of Black women, even if these portrayals provide conflicting depictions of Black women's work in the academy. On one hand, I was taking care of the college and praised by staff to my face; on the other hand, staff members later accused me of being toxic and serving as one of the main contributors to the toxic environment.

Titles Without Authority and Respect for Black Women: Just the Way It Is

In January, after the dean's continuous absence from campus due to FMLA leave, including an attempt from him to return to campus prematurely without HR clearance after FMLA, I was officially promoted to acting dean and was informed that my provost selected a number two for me, the same academic advisor without a faculty appointment or terminal degree to serve as my assistant dean, since the staff were already comfortable and familiar with working under him. While I was concerned that I would not be able to select my own leadership (no reason was given as to why), I gave my number two the benefit of the doubt, thinking that we both shared a collective vision to put self-interests aside and to do what was best for the college at the time. I figured that staff in the unit did tend to lean on his experience and pragmatism.

Unfortunately, I would learn that I would not have put the assistant dean in place had it not had my loyalty and support.

Over the course of the next semester, the state of the college did seem to be improving. Budgets that had been unbalanced were getting balanced, new initiatives were being developed, and staff seemed content with their jobs with minimal hiccups. Other than one personnel matter between two black women staff that I was required to mediate, things seemed to be improving. Several members of the campus community began reaching out expressing they were pleased with my leadership and how I have stepped in given the unusual circumstances. I had no inkling that there were troubles on the horizon until one of the Black women staff members sent an email chastising me because I offended them and other students when they overhead me refer to myself as "special" when I forgot where certain supplies were placed and had to backtrack to remember where I'd put the supplies in the first place. They noted that this offends those with disabilities, not recognizing that I had publicly disclosed two of my own disabilities to staff and the campus community. While I replied to the emailed concern apologizing for the comment and emphasized my intent to humanize myself as a leader and make myself approachable, I did not receive an email response back from her. This perhaps would foreshadow what I would later come to learn that none of the staff supported or respected my leadership even though I was appointed Acting Dean of the college.

Over the course of that semester (and academic year), I would meet one-on-one with the provost, providing updates on current projects and initiatives, for which the provost provided words of encouragement, support and affirmation. After the spring semester, the dean returned from his leave to his position, though he had been absent nearly the entire academic year due to paid medical leave he accrued while he was an employee at the University. At the end of my appointment, I submitted my professional activity report, as required, outlining my accomplishments for the year. Accomplishments ranged from increasing diversity for the institution's highest merit-based scholarship to increasing the fall to spring retention rate in the college to fundraising. While I submitted a professional evaluation, I did not receive a response, which is typical of the institution. Many deans and administrators often lament about never receiving formalized feedback. I shrugged it off and committed back to doing my original job as associate dean.

Returning and Toxicity: Investigations and Backstabbing of Black Women in Academic Spaces

Upon the dean's return, staff asked that I participate in their annual performance reviews even though I no longer supervised them suggesting that they would trust my judgment more than his since he had been absent. Multiple staff also requested that I represent the college by traveling across the state and country to present scholarship recipients with their awards, providing remarks at their various honors programs, and participating in news coverage and public relations for their local cities and school districts. They explained that because I did the effort to recruit, I should be the one to represent the college. As a result, I spent multiple weeks on the road rarely seeing the dean after he returned. Combined with the annual leave I needed to use; I was not in the office much during the first month (May) of the dean's return.

The first week of the very next month in June, the college received a visit from the provost informing us that they received several complaints about the climate of the college over the past *several months*. As a result, the provost hired an external attorney to investigate the climate and provide recommendations moving forward. While concerned with the level of seriousness that investigations take, I imagined the concerns were based on the dean's return and his refusal to work on college initiatives (he elected to work on his own personal service and campus commitments instead). His behavior also continued to be erratic and inconsistent when he returned back to campus, as he continued to show up hours late for work. Given that I was informed that this was a climate study, I did not believe I was a target of this investigation, since institutional policy requires informing the accused of a complaint, so I did not believe I needed to retain my own counsel. In hindsight, I should have retained counsel regardless of my assumptions about the intended target.

My interview with the investigator covered much of what I might expect. The investigator asked about my role, my relationship with the dean and my relationship with staff. The interview took an unsurprising turn when I was asked if I had ever made inappropriate comments in the presence of staff and students. I responded by recalling the time I called myself "special," but that's it. I was then asked if I ever said I was sick of working with whites in my unit. I responded, of course not. I then explained that I have been encouraged to talk about white privilege, racism and gender equity, and that as a scholar I write about these things in my profession; I invited the investigator to Google my name for context. I was then asked if I had concerns about the dean and if he should be removed. I simply responded with my hope for the dean to recover and get better since he had previously taken an extended leave of absence lasting most of the academic year. The investigator then asked what could be done to improve the climate and I stated that (1) the dean needs to continue his recovery in order to run the college well, and (2) staff could have more gratitude and appreciation of my work providing stability during this time. The interview concluded with me sharing the same professional activity report to which I received no previous response. While alarmed at the potential accusations, I marveled at the fact that this was the only criticism that was an accusation that I said something I did not say. I didn't think much else about potential consequences for me, but unfortunately, I would learn that was not the case.

End of My Term: Trauma and Institutional Abuse of Black Women

Two months after the investigation was announced, I received a message to meet with the provost regarding the outcome of the investigation. Upon learning that staff shared several complaints about my leadership, I was given the opportunity to resign my position; no doubt it was the right decision, as I wanted to focus on applying for promotion to full professor anyway. I was absolutely stunned—too stunned to even cry though I showed a lot of emotion about systemic racism being the cause, to which I received no rebuttal or response. The vice provost (currently interim provost at the time of this writing) also attended the meeting, but refused to look me in the eye. He never said a word. The meeting ended with me abruptly leaving the office and thanking them for their time. I moved out of my office the next day. I would later find out that they were released from work early that day to give me privacy, but many were still there when I arrived. They each filed out of the office without saying a word or making eye contact, though their smirks told it all. Not a single advocate from the office was there to offer support.

After moving out of the office, the white and female provost, at the time, and I would later devise a plan and path for return to future leadership and sponsored several leadership opportunities for me, which I greatly appreciated. While my working relationship with the then provost continues to be an amicable one, even though she is no longer the provost of my institution,

I felt deeply betrayed by staff from all sides, black women, white women, and white men, who said mostly positive things to my face, while communicating their displeasure with my leadership behind my back to my superior and to others on campus in personal and professional networks. Given the fact that I resigned from a position unjustly, I filed an equity complaint with our institution's Office of Institutional Equity (OIE) because I still felt I had not been treated fairly by my previous dean or staff. After providing my statement and hundreds of pages of evidence supporting my inequitable treatment, I was informed that I had two choices for proceeding. (1) I could launch a full investigation, or (2) at the president's request, I could provide my evidence and information for the office to produce an after-action report. Not wanting to put myself or staff through another stressful and lengthy process, I elected for an after action report with a follow up request to meet with the president, since there was no chance that I desired to be reinstated in that position; I simply wanted to clear my name and move forward.

The after action report was completed and revealed factual information from my experiences by me, evidence submitted, and a summary of concerns provided by the equity office. For example, it included evidence from emails of a white woman instructor in my former unit asking me to read the "N word" for them. I also expressed concerns about the lack of proof of me making racialized comments. In addition to my experiences, I learned from the report that their office is the office typically charged to conduct investigations such as these, not a third-party attorney, that their office was not consulted in selecting the investigator, and that their office was not consulted when a decision was made that makes the institution vulnerable to complaints of discrimination and retaliation. I also learned that the dean changed the organizational chart removing nearly all direct report responsibilities from me apart from one other Black woman. However, the job advertisement to which I applied included these responsibilities in my portfolio. I was informed that per institutional equity, they were not supposed to do this.

Apparently, the dean made a deal with the academic advisor who had been my number two so he wouldn't have to report to me and could report directly to him instead. Even prior to me working in that unit, the plan was for him to be the de facto number two, who would be part of the leadership team. To date, he has now been appointed to a permanent position as Assistant Dean of the college despite his lack of experience as a faculty member or terminal degree. I was also told by a university senior official that said the new Assistant Dean had been spreading rumors about my resignation/termination being due to an investigation in which law enforcement had been involved, therefore reinforcing stereotypes about Black women and criminality, but I digress. They wanted to maintain the good ol' boy network they had established, one that had previously led to the retirement of my white female predecessor, who never bothered to warn me about this network; and who shared her public support with the number two the weekend after my resignation celebrating on the lake with she, him, and the same Dean who is also named in Jennifer's story in the previous chapter. The report finally confirmed that I was treated differently from other administrators based on past institutional precedent.

I felt vindicated by the report and that I was finally being heard until my request to meet with the president who was the recipient of the after action report. After initially receiving no response for a meeting, I sent a follow up request and received a reply from their office that it would not result in a return to the position from which I had already resigned. I was offended by the suggestion because I did not request a return to such a toxic environment. I simply wanted to express my concerns with equity, identify a path forward to maintain professional and amicable relationships with leadership, and to understand the president's intentions for retaining me, since they had previously expressed this commitment. While my meeting with the president was pleasant, amicable, and respectful of my concerns, the meeting's focus was more on closure than structural or institutional change.

A Time to Heal: Lessons Learned from Past Trauma through Afrofuturism

In the previous chapter, Jennifer discussed the notion of *healing thyself first*, especially as it relates to healing in academic and white feminist spaces. Before I was able to move into that space for healing, and was able to use lessons learned as a means to healing myself, it is critical to examine the limits of healing through a rhetorical lens, particularly as it relates to Black women having to negotiate the many paradoxes that come with that healing, especially after the consequences and punishment in response to Black women's speech and actions. As Tamika L. Carey (2018) notes,

> Black women have experienced the results of [racial segregation] in both social as well as work realms. Even when their work as domestics required them to share close spaces with whites, black women's presence as raced and gendered bodies made

> them subject to a gaze that was enacted through "techniques of surveillance" such as close scrutiny and the threat of violence. The gaze could be calibrated through what Patricia Hill Collins describes as controlling images, or "interrelated, socially constructed" myths about black women's character and behavior, that worked to justify "the dominant group's interest in maintaining Black women's subordination" (Black Feminist Thought 57). (p. 143)

As Carey further suggests, the "technical surveillance" of Black women's speech and actions often leads to "myths about [B]lack women's character and behavior," and this in turn leads to negative and embarrassing consequences, including termination or demotion in employment (as was my case), or public apologies for public intellectuals, as was the case of her analysis of Melissa Harris Perry's discourse as a public intellectual when previously employed by MSNBC. The consequences are often no less than humiliating, and moreover reinforce double standards for Black women who have to tread lightly and behave perfectly in public discourse and in academic spaces. This moreover creates an additional paradox between expectations and reality, with Black women being surveyed by expectations.

Historically, the adverse consequences for Black women who speak up in public spaces are not new, especially in relation to healing in the public eye. Perhaps Anita Hill's (2020) experience testifying in 1991 at Supreme Court Justice Clarence Thomas' confirmation hearing to date still provides one of the most compelling examples of Black women's humiliation and healing within the public eye. Hill writes:

> Four months after I testified before Congress in October 1991, in what one commentator described as a wretched slanderous race and gender scandal, the Clarence Thomas confirmation hearing, I was at a crossroads. I had to decide whether to respond to appeals for clarity on the issue of sexual harassment or continue to try to take back my pre-hearing life as a law professor (p. ix).

Hill's book, *Believing: Our Thirty-Year Journey to End Gender Violence*, shares stories of sexual and gender-based violence through intersectional lenses that bear some similarities to our own accounts shared across Mariam's, Jennifer's, and my stories. Hill further asserts that "I see that the only way to address the troubling and persistent issue of gender violence and abuse is to take it apart and look at it step-by-step—where it comes from, how it builds—and thus understand how it's perpetuated within our culture and existing systems, or even the language we use for it" (2020, p. 14). In essence, in order to understand the racism and sexism that result from adverse consequences for

Black women is to take apart the system that enables racism and sexism to thrive.

Humiliation and consequences often point to a need for Black women's healing, a healing that often is forced to be viewed through the public eye. Carey's work also analyzes accounts of what Black women's healing looks like in public spaces, with writing and literacy often functioning as tools to facilitate that healing. More precisely, Carey defines rhetorical healing as "a set of persuasive discourses and performances writers wield to convince their readers that redressing or preventing a crisis requires them to follow the steps to ideological, communicative, or behavioral transformation the writer considers essential to wellness" (p. 5). For me, these performative functions of healing and wellness required me to write through the story as a means to help readers understand the paradoxes that Black women must negotiate as leaders and scholars in the academy.

The paradox between Black woman as caregiver and Black woman as aggressive and how I tried to negotiate the two paradoxes in relation to Black women's stereotypes also impacted my mental health. Like the women examined in Browdy's (who was discussed previously in this chapter) analysis, who needed to reconcile the paradoxes associated with this imagery as "'a positive form of coping and a protective factor for optimal mental health,' but at other times,... 'be a negative form of coping and a predictive factor for poor mental health' (p. 403)," I too had to figure out how to cope with this paradox (p. 11). Such coping and healing would involve me also taking FMLA to heal from stress, anxiety and depression. Since leaving the Honors College, I now take three different anti-anxiety and antidepressant medicines daily. More than three years after leaving this environment, I am now ready to focus more positively on a few lessons to enhance healing.

As such, the following describes lessons I have learned about doing race, gender work with administration and reflections on what it means to heal from this sort of trauma, as also related to Afrofuturistic work:

One: Believe What People Do, Not What They Say; Sisterhood Is Earned. When I applied for the position, I was *told* of the college's commitment to improve diversity, I was told they had established an intercultural competence committee and they wanted to be the college known for having real conversations about race and white privilege on this campus. However, the same folks, especially Black women claiming sisterhood, who also claimed to be the most vocal about these needs were also the same folks who expressed discomfort with me when I had these conversations. As such, I learned, lip service is for the privileged and there are consequences when Black women put their talk into action. Despite this painful lesson, I aim to think more positivity and more from an Afrofuturist lens that envisions a future of Black thought as it relates to the academy. While the concept of Afrofuturism is more directly tied to technology, applications of its theories also help us understand how we navigate the realities of a white supremacist system. As Winchester (2019) notes, "connecting Afrofuturism to human-centered design (HCD) approaches that more explicitly incorporate the concepts and considerations of equity" that enable us to locate a space for "supporting… the identification and understanding of those salient sociocultural factors that Blacks/African-Americans bring" to mainstream environments like the academy, and more specifically offices of the dean (p. 56). Put simply, if diversity, equity and inclusion are truly valued, Afrofuturistic thought suggests that this space will already exist. While I cannot change the structure of the institution to make this space exist alone, I can create an environment as a department chair of a different unit to ensure the space already exists.

Two: Institutions Are Designed to Protect Themselves, Not to Ensure Justice. While I initially thought the after action report might lead to a resolution for systemic change in campus climate since it was requested by the president, it really was simply designed as a mechanism for the institution to acknowledge that they heard my concerns and reviewed my evidence. From that review, they would maintain the status quo. It wasn't until the broader campus community began to hold leaders accountable for racial and gender equity that the campus really began taking equity and justice seriously and investing resources in pursuit of it. For me it was also a document about truth and justice. For the institution, it was a ceremonial document to acknowledge a complaint and a closed case. When we consider theories of Afrofuturism, particularly as they relate to principles of design, we must consider how we redesign systems so that they offer institutional equity and not to only protect themselves. As Manchester also explains, there are unintended consequences to design. To eliminate these negative consequences, Winchester (2019) asserts:

> As a tool, Afrofuturism facilitates the ideation and reflection on design concepts within a deeper and richer sociocultural context. As such, Afrofuturism offers (a) a means to make biases visible and (b) a methodological framework for challenging and addressing them. It is the intent that, appropriately deployed and supported, the engagement of Afrofuturism and comparable approaches will foster more inclusive and consequential design thinking that not only aids in uncovering salient

sociocultural considerations and offering a means by which to appropriately respond but, provides a framing for technological innovation (p. 60).

In other words, if institutions provided methodological processes that are designed to uncover the truth and accuracy, and if these processes have appropriate disciplinary and accountability measures designed to address institutional biases as opposed to avoiding lawsuits or institutional vulnerability, then we are truly able to address equity and justice both in institutional design and outcomes. As also noted with Jennifer and Mariam's stories, formal complaints and investigations by the institution were also used to acknowledge the existence of equity concerns without systematic changes to advance equity and inclusion. An Afrofuturistic lens, however, makes these biases visible in the pursuit of institutional change. To be clear, I have not given up on working to dismantle oppressive systems and have since received my institution's excellence in Diversity and Inclusion award; however, sharing through institutional equity complaints and in this space does help make visible institutional biases.

Three: Healing Is Difficult, Especially for Black Women and Accountability May Never Happen. After the report was received, I was expected to simply move on as the institution has closed the matter. But how does healing occur when justice as I see it does not happen? There were no wrongs acknowledged or rectified by the inflictors and they still maintain their unit positions. In addition, this sets a dangerous precedent that BIPOC women can be accused of anything that is not true (an experience that parallels the one discussed in Jennifer's chapter), but not be able to defend themselves by the same university policies and procedures applied to everyone else. By the same token, we often are not able to show any vulnerabilities and express our hurt when we are expected to move on. I was expected to return immediately to the classroom three weeks later after resignation as if nothing happened. While participating in faculty governance, I am expected to remain strong and stoic, not fully human. Under these circumstances, healing is difficult when hurt has to be censored. As applied to Afrofuturism, "through improved design processes—processes that include diverse perspectives and voices—designers increase the likelihood of improving physical, emotional, and social well-being" (Tauke et al., 2015). When design processes are made to facilitate resolution and healing, we improve the well-being of those who experience trauma. For me, the humiliation led to serious hair loss that was so bad I had to shave my head into a lower fade, and take a series of anti-depressants I currently still use.

As Mariam's chapter also suggests, accountability may never happen. With my experience, one of the greatest oppressors was rewarded by the institution with a promotion. Later in Chapter 7, we suggest that oppressors have experienced little to no accountability other than the closure of GWS: After all, they retain their positions as faculty and are permitted to go on with business as usual, similarly to how institutions function with business as usual. Even through this, we still need motivation to make visible institutional biases with the hope that accountability may happen.

Four: Even When Hurt, Never Burn Bridges with Those Who Still Hold Authority. While an Afrofuturistic lens may seem to suggest transcending the systems of structural hierarchies it also acknowledges that we will continue to work within a system where structures of racial and gender hegemony do not completely disappear. Despite this experience, I'm grateful that my personal and professional relationship with my then institution's provost did not cause irreparable harm, nor did it deny me future leadership opportunities, with whom I still have a very close working relationship. In fact, in many ways, our personal relationship was also strengthened. At the suggestion of my then provost, I was urged to apply to lead a new unit as department chair of the Institute for Intercultural and Anthropological Studies (IIAS), a unit that administers multiple interdisciplinary academic programs, including African and African American Studies, after relinquishing my joint appointment in the Department of Gender and Women's Studies due to their own racial microaggressions and refusal to support my own application for full professor. Upon earning full professor, despite the GWS faculty committee's denial of support (based on their ignorant assertion that my scholarship was not feminist and focused primarily on race) from which M. Ann was the committee chair, the provost also offered me an opportunity to develop a leadership pipeline program for BIPOC women to contribute, and to shadow her as provost for this pipeline program, since I have provost and presidential aspirations for the future. I am also grateful that I have a positive professional relationship with our institution's president and the current Honors College dean despite the previous harm done.

Concluding Remarks: Continued Healing

In many ways, sharing overlapping experiences with Jennifer and Mariam about the racism, sexism and microaggression experienced from the same institution has been therapeutic. Despite the lack of clear accountability, I am extremely grateful that we now have both organizational and intellectual spaces to collaborate as educators and scholars under the same unit; it is the sharing of these stories in this academic space that has revived our love for Black Feminism and Afrofuturistic thought. It is in this new space, IIAS that I have been able to mentor and support them as their chair, while they provide encouragement and tangible support as a leader. It is their support and generosity as faculty who respect my authority and advice that provides a safe space for Black women to lead in academic spaces. As I move forward from the past, I will express gratitude for the fact that the lessons were learned on my rise to upper senior leadership and not at the latter stages of my career. I look forward to the 30 or so years I have left in higher education and will take lessons learned about racism, integrity, and healing as I continue to lead at my current institution as both a department chair, flagship organizational chair, and campus leader for equity and justice.

· 6 ·

KEIONDRA AND OLIVIA'S PERSPECTIVES: OUTSIDERS LOOKING IN

As readers and co-conspirators, we've witnessed up close and personally the trauma experienced by Mariam, Jennifer and Staci. In this chapter, we lend our voices to speak truth to power, both as former students whom Jennifer advised; and also as teachers, scholars and activists who see how the history of white supremacy as connected to feminism, continues to work incessantly within the academy. This part of the book also highlights the nature of the relationship between Jennifer, Olivia and Keiondra and the impact of their allyship. Because the dynamic evolved beyond that of professor-student and even mentor-mentee, Keiondra and Olivia tend to refer to Jennifer by both her first name and formal title, Dr. Richardson. Yet, even as "mentor" became "ally" and "advisor" became "friend," Keiondra and Olivia still look up to Dr. Richardson as their beloved professor. In many ways both in writing and in conversation, "Dr. Richardson" simply feels more natural not just because this is the first name they knew her by but because of their pride in having Dr. Richardson as a professor.

While a significant part of this chapter documents what Keiondra and Olivia witnessed as by-standers, narratives from Keiondra and Olivia also provide insight from critical whiteness studies and research on the experience of Black academic women. Drawing from these perspectives helps Olivia and

Keiondra to contextualize their narratives. First, Keiondra describes her experience as a graduate student. She illustrates the ways in which academia delegitimizes Black women's work while attempting to undermine their success. Keiondra's story—like those of Staci, Jennifer and Mariam—is one of resilience, but also pain and struggle. Olivia then reflects on the narratives within this book, describing her perspective as not only a friend but also a white woman. We (Keiondra and Olivia) end the chapter in dialogue with one another about our memories of a particularly salient attack on Dr. Richardson. We have chosen to present this as a dialogue for symbolic, preferential, and practical reasons.

On a practical level, it makes sense to recount these events in dialogue form because we experienced and witnessed them alongside each other, responding and reacting as a unified front. If we were to present two distinct narratives, they would be anything but distinct and would, in fact, mirror each other almost exactly. Beyond practicalities, we simply prefer to work together and have done so since forming our friendship. In this way, the dialogue format also acts as a symbol of our commitment to collaboration and one of the larger goals of this book: to model allyship among Black and white women. In short, we believe there is more to be gained in collaboration.

Keiondra's Story

While Jennifer, Mariam and Staci have noted that Olivia and I served as allies on this journey, contemporaneously, I experienced my own harm inflicted by the very department to which Jennifer attempted to transfer. The harm I endured coupled with watching Jennifer's experiences with both GWS and her intended transfer department served as catalyst for my escape from academia. Going into my doctoral program, I was already well aware of the harm and trauma that exists in academic spaces for Black women, especially after completing both my bachelor's and master's degrees at predominately white Midwest institutions. However, after revealing my concerns to my potential colleagues, I reasoned that going into a professed social justice-oriented department would in some ways diminish the harm. I quickly discovered that, quite simply, the harm can shape shift.

In August of 2015, I entered a doctoral program at the same institution as my coauthors. In order to fund my education, I applied for two funding sources at the institution—a graduate college fellowship and a departmental teaching assistantship. I was awarded both and decided upon the fellowship opportunity. This was a one-year, full fellowship with the possibility of yearly renewal up to a maximum of three additional years. Requirements for the fellowship included registering for at least six credit hours per fall and spring term and three for summer sessions. I also was required to serve as a doctoral associate at a maximum of 10 hours per week in the areas of research, service, or teaching. Relative to the departmental teaching assistantship (which required 20 hours per week teaching) the fellowship allowed for fewer weekly hours and more time to focus on my studies. It also allowed me to explore my research and service ambitions. In addition, the fellowship opportunity provided students of color with supportive groups to help navigate graduate studies at the institution.

I was advised that as long as I maintained a good academic standing (3.0 GPA) and worked the required 10 hours as a doctoral associate each week at the discretion of my department, subsequent yearly funding was guaranteed through four complete years. The median length of time to complete a life sciences degree in 2020 was 6.9 years (Coursera, 2022). The graduate college as well as my department told me during my first year that if I needed additional funding (after the four-year fellowship), I could again apply for the departmental teaching assistantship. I also learned that this particular graduate college funding did not hinder access to departmental funding opportunities. I specifically asked questions related to these issues before starting the program because, as a first-generation college student, the availability of financial support for my entire five-year timeline was important for me to complete the process.

In my first year, I was given a position as a research assistant working at a race relations institute on campus. I immersed myself in the work of the institute, particularly their investments in community organizations. As I began my work within the institute, I realized the director, a white man, believed that race was not as important as class inequality. He also did not understand my desire to study and pursue Black feminist-based research and activism. However, he had extensive connections with community service agencies, and I enjoyed the opportunity to work within the community through those connections. Also, he allowed me free range in terms of how I used my 10 hours. I decided to invest in two community organizations aimed at assisting Black and other women of color in the community, specifically addressing issues of incarceration and substance abuse. I deeply enjoyed this work and invested many more hours helping these organizations with programing, grant acquisition, research, and community initiatives.

This work was directly aligned with my identification as a Black feminist, an identity strengthened by mentorship under Jennifer, who stressed the importance of intersectional perspectives of community issues, while emphasizing the need to blend theory with practical applications. I fully embodied that energy in my academic pursuits. I quickly learned that the local community, particularly communities of color, did not have the best relationship with the college. Nor did they possess a high regard of the college and its involvement with local communities. I understood these sentiments, as I watched my classmates and faculty theorize on end about social problems, despite boasting little to no direct community action or application.

Throughout my program it became apparent that the community work I was doing was viewed as lesser than the theoretical pursuits of my white peers, as illustrated by my experiences with the annual review process. First, my program requires graduate students to undergo an annual review, consisting of submitting a current curriculum vitae, a course timeline, and a succinct one-page narrative regarding our academic accomplishments. Academic accomplishments as outlined by the department consisted of things such as completed coursework, high GPAs, exam area completion, conference presentations, grant acquisitions, additional training in our fields, and service to the profession. The Central Graduate Committee of the department used annual review to inform students of our progress in the program and decide if students are eligible for department funding. They assessed whether students were making excellent progress, acceptable progress with concerns, unacceptable progress, or whether our performance required dismissal from graduate school.

During my time in the program, I consistently held a high GPA (3.9). I also stayed on track for the course timeline, presented at both regional and national conferences each year, and enrolled in more courses than required. Additionally, I taught courses at another university, continued extensive work in the community, and became involved with a new departmental wrongful conviction program. Despite providing information on various ways in which I exceeded the criteria for excellent progress in the program, for my first three years, I consistently received "Acceptable Progress with concerns," although the listed concerns were not applicable to my nonacademic chosen path.

Although the Annual Review process was subjective, it was invalidating to be exceeding program expectations, yet consistently receiving reviews that were below other students. The lack of investment the department had for service work was apparent. Perhaps if I were invested in mainstream theoretical pursuits, extensive academic publishing, and commitment to the department specifically, I would have received excellent reviews. In addition, those reviews might have manifested as accolades and departmental awards that other students received for what appeared like the bare minimum in comparison.

Despite the lack of recognition for my work within my department, I continued to find value in community engagement. In those spaces I was awarded multiple awards and accolades and overall found my community. In 2019, I was in my final year of funding through the fellowship. With the encouragement of the department graduate director, student advisor, and my dissertation chair, who were all white women, I decided to apply for departmental funding for my upcoming fifth and final year. Each colleague told me that I was practically guaranteed funding through the department due to the fact I had completed over the required amount of course work, defended both of my area exams "with distinction," earning the rare honor of no rewrites, exceeded the required GPA and was ready to defend my dissertation proposal. Accordingly, I submitted my materials in December 2018.

In February of 2019 I was told that I received excellent progress and that I was being awarded the departmental teaching effectiveness award and all-university teaching award (although I was not fond of teaching, I was good at it). However, I was never told if funding decisions were made. I asked other students and faculty if decisions had been made, and people stated they were unsure if funding letters had gone out. Finally, on March 21, 2019, I emailed the graduate director specifically to ask about funding and was told I did not receive funding for the upcoming year. She offered a few outside funding resources to check into as well as adjunct opportunities through the department and wished me luck. I remember being confused, because she and multiple other women in the department encouraged me to apply, and I also knew that I met all the outlined criteria to receive the funding. Though frustrated, I was not altogether surprised by the outcome, because often goal posts are moved before Black people can benefit, as illustrated by the University of North Carolina's denial of tenure to the Pulitzer-Prize winning journalist Nikole Hannah-Jones. Additionally, I realized later that when I was asking my mostly white peers about funding decisions, they had lied about their status, claiming they had not received their funding letters when it was clear they had been disseminated.

I decided to turn my anger and frustration into action. Shortly after I inquired about the lack of funding to the department graduate director, notes from the recent Central Graduate Committee meeting were sent through the acting vice president of the Graduate Student Association (GSA), which acts on behalf of graduate students. In the notes, he mentioned that the Central Graduate Committee had decided that all students should only receive four years of funding, regardless of whether it was through the college or department. At that time, I was the only student who was slated to receive funding from the Graduate College, and transitioned to funding by the Department of Sociology. I also was the only one who did not study mainstream sociology. Typically, however, students who receive funding through my fellowship and the college are students of color. Given this knowledge, I decided to draft an email to the graduate director asking for specifics about why I did not receive funding, despite meeting program criteria. She simply asked for an in person meeting later that week to discuss my concerns. Looking back, I can assume this call for an in-person discussion was to avoid written documentation.

At the meeting I let her know that the seemingly new rules directly impacted students of color negatively. I also inquired as to why this was suddenly an issue, especially given my circumstances. She responded by saying that the department wanted to ensure that everyone got equal amounts of funding and making it four years only ensured that for everyone. She also stated that they base decisions on who needs the most assistance in terms of where they were in the program. Those with more years left to complete were priority in the funding hierarchy. She again offered other resources, but was not able to meet or challenge my inquiries directly. In fact, she teared up at my assertions that the new rule disadvantaged students of color specifically. I decided to take the issue to the sociology GSA.

The GSA called on faculty and the Central Graduate Committee to outline specifically how they assess funding decisions for students. Unfortunately, although GSA talked big, it very much felt as though they did not want to rock the boat on my behalf. Faculty consistently sent limited responses to our calls for funding transparency and after a while the issue was dropped. It was apparent that because the issue did not affect the majority of students (mostly white), it simply was not a priority issue. Overall, it was apparent during my graduate school program that my areas of interest and pursuits were not valued, and therefore I was not valued. The brazen change of rules that disadvantaged me solidified this notion in my mind. I finished my degree within five years and "with distinction" at every junction.

Finding a community outside of academia and allies within (Olivia and Jennifer at the time) helped me to remain vested in my interests and walk my path despite the lack of support, recognition, and direct challenge. In the years since finishing my program, I have reflected on the experience, particularly while co-writing this book. It would be remiss of me not to mention that I maintained high performance during the program, despite losing both my grandmother (March 2018) and father (December 2018) in the same year of my area exams (February and November 2018). Admittedly when asked to write this book, I had blocked out much of the trauma I experienced during my graduate program. Reflecting on the harm I endured, and the experiences Jennifer had both in GWS and my department, I realized they were the final push I needed in determining that academia and its toxicity towards Black women was not something I wanted to navigate any longer. I am happy to have earned my degree and taken it to bolster community organizations (albeit they are not without their own challenges with white supremacist and mainstream feminist ideologies).

Olivia's Story

As a white woman, I have discovered how, in many ways, the history and evolution of white feminism plays out explicitly in the stories that Mariam, Jennifer and Staci shared regarding their experiences in the academy. Although Keiondra did not work in a gender studies department, the lip service the graduate students and faculty offered on equity and antiracism is also characteristic of white feminism. This is not all that surprising as white feminism was essentially institutionalized through the establishment of women's studies and the inception of feminism into pre-existing academic programs (e.g., history, languages and literatures, sociology, etc.). Those working to bring feminism into the academy thought of women's studies, and affiliated departments, as the "academic arm" of the women's movement (Ginsberg, 2008). As one component of a larger body (so to speak), the academic arm was clearly affected by the problems that riddled the other organs and extremities. Feminists who made their way into higher education brought along with them their prioritization of white women's standpoints, their animosity toward women who sought to challenge their singular and banal analysis of power, and their limited understanding of "women's issues."

In their introductory essay to the book *Antagonizing White Feminism,* Chaddock and Hinderliter (2019) point out that some of the fiercest defenders of white supremacy within feminism come from women's studies and women's studies adjacent programs. They argue that these spaces "hypocritically claim to offer women solace, advocacy, safety, solidarity, advancement and political salience" (p. xiii) while exercising their power over women who exist at the intersections of race, ethnicity, gender identity, class, and sexual orientation. We clearly see this in Staci, Jennifer and Mariam's stories. Just as white abolitionists-turned-suffragists expelled Black women from their "Votes for Women" campaigns, professors and program directors created hostile environments for Staci, Jennifer, and Mariam while touting their commitment to intersectional feminism, diversity, equity and inclusion. In the process, they elicited (consciously or not) support from other whites to protect white supremacy.

DiAngelo (2018) refers to white solidarity as an "unspoken agreement" by white people to disregard instances of racism that will not only protect other whites from racial discomfort but ensure the maintenance of white supremacy. We see this in Mariam's story, where administration and other faculty worked together to keep the power concentrated among the individuals willing to weaponize their white womanhood in service of the status quo. We also see this in Staci's story in her description of how the Honors College actively worked to live up to its reputation as a "for whites only" space.

As a graduate student, I witnessed this first-hand in both the women's studies department and in another department I worked in at the same university. I was a young white feminist who, like so many other young white women, came to understand the limits of my agency through the resistance I met in formal institutions (Reger, 2014). I was naive about how institutions functioned and how white supremacy and sexism manifested in those institutions. In trying to conspire with Keiondra (and others) against the discrimination she experienced, I witnessed how, as a form of misogynoir, college officials constantly moved goal posts and offered empty promises. Keiondra would achieve something and the bar for recognition would shift. She would receive accolades from those she worked with directly while being snubbed for departmental awards. For example, despite producing essays for area exams that were so impressive her committees formally recognized them as distinct from that of her peers, the department exploited her service to the community, all the while using her investment in public sociology and Black feminist methods as a reason to withhold accolades. Once, I worked with our mentor in the department (Lauren) to put together a detailed list of reasons as to why Keiondra should receive a highly prestigious award for "service to the department." Rather than acknowledge Keiondra, the award was not given to anyone that year. This was the first time, to my knowledge, nobody received the annual award.

Up until the end of our graduate career, Keiondra and I coordinated responses to the antics. We would go into meetings and events with a game plan on how we would hold others accountable. We planned these "callouts" together and I would practice my plan of what to say with her while she would listen for places to strengthen, soften, and tweak. She would read email drafts and we would revise them together. We made a good team, but we felt alone in our struggle and eventually the goal became "let's just get the [expletive] out of here." The clearly discriminatory funding policy Keiondra described previously was probably the last straw for both of us. I cannot recall a single department event (outside of required meetings) we attended after that. It was at this same time I was becoming more involved in the gender and women's studies department. Initially, I went in hoping for a new atmosphere, excited to work alongside Dr. Richardson. What I found was something more toxic than I could imagine.

When I first started working in the department, Dr. Richardson had given me a gentle warning to be careful about what I shared with Karen. This transition strengthened our relationship such that it would evolve beyond student-professor. As time went on, and she began to trust me more, I became privier to what was going on "behind the scenes." In women's studies meetings and gatherings where Jennifer was not present, I recall feeling almost baited by Karen to bad-mouth her. She knew Jennifer was my advisor and that I had come to the department on her reference. Why would she assume my allegiance would be to her (Karen), some random lady who oversaw my graduate assistantship? Was it whiteness? Indeed, she must have regarded me as a potential white woman ally.

During my last year in the department, I signed up for a book club led by Karen. As a department sponsored event, it promised a stipend of $100, a free book (if needed), and at least two hours of awkward conversation. The book up for discussion was Brittney Cooper's *Eloquent Rage*. At this point, I had been in the department for a full year so I was well aware of the abuse Jennifer experienced at the hands of "my boss." "Ironic choice," I thought but signed up anyway.

The day of, I showed up ready to talk with some fellow white ladies about Cooper's take on feminism. This, of course, happened but so too did some Olympic-level bending over backwards to avoid any real conversation about the elephant in the room—whiteness. We talked about antisemitism, we talked about exclusion of lesbians in feminist spaces, we talked about our students, we talked about anti-porn and anti-sex positive feminists. We talked about everything but Cooper's take on white womanhood and we certainly did not talk about the uncomfortable truth that the only people who showed up to a discussion of a piece written by a Black woman were white. We did talk about Jennifer's absence, however. I remember the conversation going something like this:

> "I was expecting a lot more people to show up today," said Karen. As Karen spoke, there were additional nods and murmured affirmations from around the table. "Olivia, have you heard from Dr. Richardson? I expected her to be here," she added. "Yeah, she's not planning on coming. I don't think she ever planned on coming as far as I know," I responded. "Well, that's interesting," Karen said, "because she took one of the books." Never mind the fact that Jennifer was using the book that semester in her Black Feminisms course.

By this point, Karen was well aware I was not going to be baited by her attempts to malign Dr. Richardson. In the previous year, she would make a point to stop by my office, ask how I was doing and how my dissertation was going. It felt like she wanted to create opportunities for me to talk negatively about Jennifer and took every opportunity to undermine my advisor's expertise. There was a palpable shift in her demeanor when I would speak lovingly about my mentor. She would lash out, dismiss, or set aside any affirming comments (no matter how benign) about Jennifer or how I was benefiting from her as a mentor. At this same book club, there was a moment when the conversation began to shift toward the relationship between white and Black women. The rather irrelevant question as to whether or not we as white women could ethically engage with Black feminism came up and, feeling as if this was probably the most useless conversation we could have surrounding Cooper's critique of white feminism, I piped in:

> I don't know, I think this is a debate white women go back and forth about a lot. Dr. Richardson helped me come to understand my role as a student of Black feminism and gave me the language to think about it as a "user's guide" or like an "owner's manual" for how to do feminism. We can use it as a way to map out a path forward

and figure out how to be better feminists but I'm not sure it's as important to Cooper's discussion of how white women weaponize our power.

To clarify, this felt like an irrelevant conversation not because it was unimportant; rather, it felt irrelevant because whether white women can or should identify with Black feminism is really beside the point when the actual, real-life Black women in our community are not safe. Predictably, Karen scoffed at my having learned a valuable thing from a Black woman she hated. She looked around the table at the other white women and replied: "A *user's guide*? I don't know, I think that wording—'owner's manual'—is an interesting choice of words. Don't you think that raises concerns about you owning Black feminism? Like, who's owning who here if we take Black feminism as an 'owner's manual'? I just think 'owner' and 'user' is a problematic choice of words here." More nods and murmured affirmations in response.

I replied, "I think you know what I mean. It's a way of thinking about how we can make ourselves useful." It was satisfying to snap at her. Looking back, however, it was a counterproductive response. First, it was a clear exercise of the privileges I reap from my social position. Radical, intersectional feminism is about dismantling the systems of power that produce privilege/inequality such that no group is unfairly advantaged over another (see hooks, 1984). Within this perspective, privilege is not something that can be used for good. Exercises in privilege are exercises in the inequitable distribution of power. I was not stereotyped as combative and antagonistic and my snippy response did not result in any real repercussions. Had I been a woman of Color (particularly a Black woman), I would have likely been accused of acting aggressively toward my supervisor (see Harris-Perry, 2012) and may have faced both formal and informal sanctions. Moreover, it just was not a productive way to respond to Karen's misbehavior. The more productive thing to do would have been to publicly call out Karen for attempting to mock a Black woman colleague, thereby demonstrating that intersectional feminism is not something we do just when Black women are in the room and not just another space for white women to mechanize their privilege. Instead, I snapped and while it felt good, it was short sighted and reactionary and an exercise in power that cannot be justified in intersectional approaches to women's liberation.

This seems to me another aspect of white solidarity. Of course, white solidarity manifests as it is described by DiAngelo—white people closing ranks around white people in an effort to ensure we remain centered (2018). But over the course of my life as a white woman, I have come to recognize my own complacency, my tendency toward "flighty-ness" and distraction, as additional manifestations of white solidarity. In expecting like-mindedness, benevolence, and support from other whites I am prone to letting my guard down around my people. I fail to recognize individual white feminists as potential sources of harm and am too quick to relax. I find myself easily caught off guard when white feminists do what white feminists do (i.e., all the themes, behaviors, etc. that have been discussed throughout this book) and often do not think of the right thing to say until hours later when I am reliving the interaction in my head or until I share the story with a friend. Unprepared and caught off-guard, I fall back on the privileges attached to my social position by snapping and producing half-baked attempts at accountability.

Critical whiteness scholars would probably characterize this as a failure to develop "racial stamina." Racial stamina is a concept used in whiteness studies to describe white peoples' tendency toward stress, anger, defensiveness, and discomfort around conversations about race (DiAngelo, 2016). While this is a useful concept for making sense of whites' negative reactions to these types of conversations, I do not believe it adequately describes some whites' failure. Or, perhaps it does not adequately characterize *my* failure to prepare for confrontation with other whites. When I reflect on some of the events already described here, it's clear to me that I lacked vigilance, and if there is anything a co-conspirator must be it is vigilant. I look back at all of the diversity workshops and inclusion seminars I attended and wonder why "stay alert!" did not spearhead our lessons. To be an effective co-conspirator and intersectional feminist one really does need to practice mindfulness and remain focused, not letting the status quo of white supremacy become unremarkable. This feels particularly important in spaces like academia, where white feminists have become experts at weaponizing institutions against Black women. We (Keiondra and Olivia) witnessed this first hand as Jennifer tried to make her way out of the gender and women's studies department.

Keiondra and Olivia in Conversation

In one of our last years as graduate students, we were rather involved in the effort to get Dr. Richardson out of gender and women's studies and into the department where we were working on our doctoral degrees. Because we were both very close with Jennifer, the three of us were in constant conversation about the transfer process; at no point did we keep information from Jennifer.

Our department housed the same discipline as that of Jennifer's terminal degree but, as we came to discover, the faculty there had already begun to close ranks against Jennifer. Jennifer describes some of this in her story where she explains how Karen and M. Ann briefed colleagues in the receiving department about Jennifer before the transfer process had even started. Because this conflict was so formative for both of us, we have a dialogue about that experience in what remains of this chapter.

Olivia: My first memory of this whole ordeal doesn't actually start with Dr. Richardson; it starts with one of the professors (Lauren) in our graduate program. Looking back, I should have known it would be a mess. I remember Lauren walking past the kitchenette where I was making coffee, stopping when she noticed me and then pulling me aside to explain (in whispered tones, I should add) that Dr. Richardson was going to attempt to transfer into our department as a tenure-track faculty member. My first reaction—which was elation—was immediately replaced by anxiety and apprehension. I was elated because you and I had been jumping through tons of hoops to find ways to get course credit for our work with Dr. Richardson, and her transfer meant we would no longer have to justify how our activity with her was relevant to our doctoral program. Elation quickly faded when Lauren explained that the transfer would not happen if the graduate students were not willing to put up a fight for her.

Keiondra: I remember you coming to tell me pretty close after the conversation. Looking back, Lauren felt supportive of what we wanted to accomplish. I also felt excited about her potential transfer, because Dr. Richardson was helping to develop our understanding and engagement with Black feminisms. The department in general really needed what Dr. Richardson had to offer in my opinion: an intersectional perspective but also fresh and engaging courses and conversations! I felt the other grad students would absolutely advocate for her transfer. I also thought that because two other faculty members had just experienced seemingly easy transfers into the department, this should be a no brainer.

Olivia: The department definitely would have benefited from Jennifer's transfer. The race and ethnicity area in the doctoral program was really starting to dwindle away. The last two hires were expected to be race and ethnicity scholars (they weren't) and one of the few professors affiliated with the area had just retired. If you will recall, Keiondra, this was all happening while demand for more race-centered classes and professors were increasing among the graduate students. After I got the heads up from Lauren, I told everyone I ran into that Dr. Richardson was trying to join the department. There was a lot of ambivalence about the previous two transfers being tasked with teaching graduate-level courses despite them not having a degree in our discipline. So, support for a race and ethnicity scholar with an in-house degree was high. More than that, the previous transfers had not even bothered to reach out to graduate students during or after the transfer process.

Knowing that we would need to organize–per Lauren's advice–I reached out to the president of our GSA and began trying to coordinate a meet and greet between the graduate students and Jennifer. Beyond the graduate students' frustration with the previous transfers, I just remember a lot of people being really interested in Jennifer after hearing about the work you and I were doing with her. They were genuinely excited at the prospect of her joining our department. Within a relatively short period of time the transfer process started to devolve. Every now and then, another professor we both worked with started "warning" me about working with Jennifer. She implied that Jennifer would struggle to get tenure and that I would be putting my area exams and dissertations in jeopardy by appointing her to my committees. She belittled her research—referring to it as "unpublishable." This is another place where I really feel like I lost focus and did not practice mindful vigilance. My response was reactionary. I lashed out, said I would not change my committee member and that I liked working with Jennifer. That would have been an ideal time to call out her white feminism. After the two other immediate transfers, I really did not think they could deny Jennifer.

Keiondra: I naively thought that Jennifer's transfer would be pretty smooth. Dr. Richardson fit perfectly into everything the graduate students were calling for in the department, and from my perspective, the transfer process seemed pretty easy. During the 2016/2017 school year I served as Vice President of the department Graduate Student Association (GSA) and in that role attended faculty meetings on behalf of grad students. I was privy to the transfers of the two faculty you mentioned. While I did not get to sit in on final deliberations or vote for candidates, I was able to hear their job talks and give my feedback before leaving for the faculty discussion and vote. The first transfer candidate job talk was with a white man who held a terminal degree in Anthropology. I recall his talk vividly because it was the day after Trump was elected. The overall spirit in the room was pretty low and because of that he decided to have a conversation, essentially about what enabled Trump to be elected. He focused on explaining that working class white people bought into Trump's rhetoric around immigration and his appeal to their grievances about being left behind by globalization. To put it frankly, I was not impressed. I saw a white man that subverted the process, and also centered white feelings, negating the devastating impact for women and people of color. Also, it seemed he felt like this was all a matter of formality and he was a shoe-in for the transfer. Other white male faculty seemed really engaged in the "talk." I remember at some point a heavy focus on working-class white Ohioans. Afterwards, I spoke to Lauren, who was similarly unimpressed but let me know that the transfer was going to be approved.

That's when I realized the transfer process was very informal. Gloria (the faculty member that fled GWS, mentioned in Jennifer and Mariam's narratives) initiated the transfer process in 2017, but hers was not as informal. She did not meet with graduate students as you mentioned. She did give a traditional job talk. I do not remember exactly what her talk entailed; however, she had been a clinical practitioner before teaching, and at the point of transfer, she only had four years left until retirement. Also, following her talk there were a lot of questions from faculty that felt as if they were trying to poke holes or harshly critique her work, which they failed to do with the white male faculty member. This furthered my feelings about the bias lobbed at those considered feminist researchers in the department. Ultimately, they decided to accept Gloria on a two-year probationary period. I found that odd, considering the lax nature of the previous transfer, and the fact that the chair of our department at the time said the job talks were really just formalities for transfer. I should share that while I do not remember the specifics of her talk, I did feel she did not fit what we needed in the department at the time. However, comparing the two transfers, it was clear no formal process existed, unless faculty wanted it to exist.

Olivia: Admittedly, this is where I become incredibly confused about the actual transfer process. Some of this, of course, is because as graduate students we were not involved in the decision-making and faculty did not take time to explain to us the ins and outs of these procedures. Given that our department was entirely focused on preparing students for tenure-track positions, this seems ironic at best. To this day I am unsure of how things *should* have gone down with Jennifer. What I do know, however, is that the experience of Dr. Richardson was very different from that of the previous two transfers. I know this because I met with one of the newly transferred professors during the thick of the transfer process. At this point I already knew Jennifer was receiving pushback from the other faculty, as she was told by the Dean of CAS and the chair of our department that she should set up individual meetings with each faculty member in the department. This also became clearer when Jennifer told me she was keeping a list of yeses, noes and maybes. That my mentor had to keep a roster of whose support she could count on and whose she could not was not a good sign. "Why is this even a problem?" I remember thinking. "We let in those other two and they are far less qualified to teach discipline-specific courses."

The newly transferred person I met with was in fact a maybe. Jennifer was unsure of whether she had his vote and I decided to meet with him under the guise of considering him as a dissertation committee member. When I sat down in his office and explained the dissertation topic, he asked who else I was talking to about the dissertation. I mentioned their names, including Jennifer's. To my surprise, he immediately began expressing concern with how her transfer was being handled. It did not make sense to him that his transfer (and that of the several other faculty members who had come over from his department over the years) were mere matters of protocol while this felt like an all-out battle. According to this person, he—along with Lauren—were some of the lone dissenters in department meetings about the transfer. He implied that Jennifer's request was treated like an unjustified, attempted invasion from an outsider. "Some of the other faculty—I won't say who—are worried that if we approve her transfer then other people will flock to the department." This felt completely asinine to me and, according to this person, it was. "She's a tenure-track, unionized faculty member. She could request a transfer to teach bowling and they'd have to give it to her for at least two years," he said. I remember thinking, "well what are *you* going to do about it?" Censoring myself, I instead asked, "what can be done about it?" He shrugged his shoulders and said something to the effect of, "I don't know. I wish I could do more but I'm new here." Looking back and as a tenure-track faculty now myself, I know how ludicrous it was for him to suggest he was powerless. As faculty we do not have a ton of power but if you are a tenured professor who is both white and male you can rest assured, at the very least, that your resistance and dissent is protected. Because of how awful the response was from other faculty though, he felt supportive at the time. The bar was clearly low.

Keiondra: As graduate students committed to intersectional feminist analysis, we really did not have many faculty aligned with our interests, which is how we became involved with Jennifer. We were tasked with constructing three committees (two for area exams and one for the dissertation) from faculty outside our interests. I had discussions with multiple faculty myself, trying to figure out who might best align with my research goals. In my discussions, a lot of faculty members talked up the importance of service, yet I did not see that in application. One such white male faculty member, Jason, often started dialogue with students referring to himself as a "poor dumb school boy" discussing how he stumbled into academia after his teachers continued to see something special in him. At the beginning of my program, he was one of the people at the top of my list because he was often critical of academia and gate keeping. However, as I became more critical in my analysis of systems, I soon saw him as another person who talked a big game with nothing to show for his critiques outside of publications. I was affirmed in my suspicions in one of his courses, where we discussed the lack of representation of certain groups in academia and our department specifically. When both you and I challenged the racial representation in the department and diversity of research areas, specifically Black feminism, his retort was simply that he had not had a Black feminist's resume cross his desk. In that moment it was clear he did not get it, and his discussion felt performative.

Another faculty member at the top of my list of potential mentors was a woman of color in the department. I was impressed with her research and teaching. We grew fairly close, as she was interested in my dissertation topic. She began to share a lot of her own personal struggles in the department as a woman of color with me. There was a "resist" sign on her desk and she let me know it was a reminder to her that she was capable of navigating the bull that comes with academia for her as a woman of color and qualitative researcher. I really admired her after some of those conversations and was leaning towards putting her on some of my committees. Then, fast forward to Jennifer's transfer and I learned she was on Jennifer's "no" list because she practically ran from her in the hallway. I was shocked, especially given what she had shared about the hostility she also faced in the department.

Olivia: Because of my own ignorance, I assumed this person would welcome and support Jennifer's transfer just as we did. I was such a huge fan of this person that their lack of support for Dr. Richardson was kind of shocking. At the time, however, my understanding of racism was not very nuanced. I thought of it as something all people of color experienced in the same way. I did not understand the relationship between anti-Blackness and other forms of racism against non-Black groups or how white supremacy leveraged anti-Blackness against racialized groups as a mechanism of control. At a certain point I remember just feeling totally gaslit. How could this person—who championed intersectionality in the classroom–literally run away from a

Black woman candidate rather than give her the time of day? How could any of the professors look us in the eye after failing to show up for Dr. Richardson?

Then there was the total lack of organized response from the GSA. It was around this time I started to adopt the mantra "stop being surprised" as a way to stay grounded because it felt like everyone was lying to us—vowing support then dropping the ball, claiming solidarity and then totally failing to show up. This is when we realized that the graduate students did not actually want to mess around with Black feminism—they wanted to tokenize it. They did not want to do the work of intersectional feminism; to conspire against institutions and protect the Black women within them, not for the sake of saviorism but because they understood the relationship between the exploitation of Black women in academia and their own. They were quick to demonstrate outrage or "release a statement," but it felt like they viewed anti-racism and anti-sexism as a thing they should perform so they would not look bad. This took a while for both of us to grasp. Looking back, it was kind of like a scene from a cartoon where two kids go to tell off the school bullies thinking they have a big crowd of people behind them only to find out that the other kids scrammed as soon as their backs were turned. Then, after all their big talk about wanting to bring in a Black feminist, they actually held a GSA meeting to discuss the "rigor" of our area exams. They raised questions about "certain exams" where people could "build their own reading lists" and "work with committee members to craft their own questions." They were clearly referring to our exam with Jennifer as a committee member—the gender and feminism exam—where historically, the exam is treated as a collaboration between mentors and mentees. This type of collaborative work is just part of feminist sociology. I remember saying something like "This is obviously about our exams, exams we both passed *with distinction*. You want to create your own reading lists? You want to collaborate with your mentors? Then come on over and join us because that's how we do it but you have to join the feminists and what you'll find out is that it's actually *more* work. We're doing more reading, more research, and more studying because we don't have the professors in this department to make our reading lists for us. If you don't want to do that work then stick with your people and keep doing things the same." This was so clearly an attempt to delegitimize the work we were doing with Jennifer after they all talked big game about wanting a Black feminist professor. They told on themselves; they wanted a token and did not believe in the work.

Keiondra: That last year of the program, I felt overwhelming disappointment. Disappointment in the university, the department faculty, and my grad school colleagues. All the experiences I have discussed, and the many left out, culminated in understanding that I, (and other Black women like Dr. Richardson) were not supported, appreciated or valued outside of making spaces *look* diverse. There was no understanding or adaptation for the way service is immensely important to Black communities and academics. Beginning to work with Dr. Richardson is one of the biggest blessings of my graduate experience because I got to engage deeply with Black feminisms both in theory and practice. What we were learning about Black feminisms, we were also experiencing in real time. Olivia, you are speaking truth when you highlight that oftentimes white colleges and mentors do not truly understand how our fates are tied. While I was never surprised by anything that occurred, I desperately wanted things to be different. I hoped that at least graduate students on a large scale would go further than tokenizing intersectionality and my existence. However, I discovered that true co-conspirators, ones like you, who understand the interconnectedness of oppression, are truly hard to come by.

Conclusion

When we were in the thick of our graduate programs, we did not think of ourselves as "doing" Black feminism. Even when we actively attempted to resist the discrimination and exploitation of Black women, we did not connect our actions to Black feminist praxis. Yet, one of the central tenets of Black feminism is that systems of oppression must be challenged through activism (Collins, 1990). In reflecting on this time and recounting our experiences, we now think of it as a "trial by fire." It was an experience that tested our grit and challenged our commitment to Black feminism. As co-conspirators who were experts in Black feminist theory, yet also graduate students who were witnesses, Patricia Hill Collins's concept of "outsiders-within" resonated with us.

Patricia Hill Collins (1986) concept of "outsiders-within" argues that Black women sociologists occupy a particular position in the academy that produces a distinctive voice and epistemological standpoint. This distinctive voice seeks to uplift the voices of Black women that are often silenced, challenge oppression through activism, and empower Black women in the face of intersecting oppressions (1986). While we were studying the intellectual tradition of Black feminism, we were also witnessing (and for Keiondra, experiencing) Black women's "outsider within status" in the academy.

As students of Black feminism, we could describe what was going on in scholarly terms, we could write about it and we spent hundreds of hours reading about it. In this way, we were insiders—we had the frame to make sense of the events we described in this chapter. But as graduate students and witnesses we were often on the outside. We were outside of the spaces where decisions were made and we felt alienated from our department. Our acquired expertise was not valued in the same ways as those of our mainstream counterparts. However, we knew what needed to be done, but as fledgling intersectional feminists without many allies of our own, we struggled to turn our plan into action.

It was our collaboration, built upon the tenets of Black feminisms, however, which gave meaning to our experiences, disappointing as they may have been. While our attempts to get our mentor the recognition and respect she deserved were not wholly successful, the process strengthened our relationship with Dr. Richardson which in turn impacted our work. Keiondra's research, for instance, examined the collateral impacts of the carceral state on the lives of Black women acting as caregivers for individuals who are incarcerated while Olivia turned her gaze to white feminists in her community. Both projects incorporated Black feminist standpoints, departed from a commitment to praxis, and would not have been possible were it not for our collaboration with Dr. Richardson. This is not to say "look, everything turned out okay!" because everything did not turn out okay. Successful dissertations and fulfilling collaborations do not assuage the effects of the onslaught of misogynoir experienced by Keiondra and Jennifer, and the dearth of accountability of individual actors and the institution. It is to reiterate, however, that our fates are bound and there are benefits to be reaped by acting accordingly.

What unites the narratives in this book is the collective standpoint discussed by Collins. These stories demonstrate how Black feminist standpoints enrich our understanding of how power works and manifests within the context of academia. Emerging at the intersection of racism and sexism, they necessarily complicate single-axis analyses of oppression that would have us look to one system of power. In addition, the narratives highlight the distinctive voice discussed by Collins, uplifting Black feminist work and creating spaces of empowerment among each other. Our hope is that in telling these stories and reflecting on the experiences, we create conditions where Black women and co-conspirators no longer feel like outsiders-within; And that we now demand accountability.

· 7 ·

CONCLUSION: SISTERHOOD, ACTION STEPS AND ACCOUNTABILITY

"As long as women are using class or race power to dominate other women, feminist sisterhood cannot be fully realized."

–bell hooks, Feminist Theory From Margin to Center

This chapter is about accountability, mutual struggle, and collective action in cross-race alliances among women of varying backgrounds. It is our position that while cross-race solidarity is key to women's liberation, the orthodox understanding of sisterhood, which was born out of white feminism, is limited. Thus, in the first part of the chapter, we focus on Olivia, our white co-conspirator whom we consider an expert in white feminist politics, behaviors, and thought. We also consider her a practitioner of Black feminist thought, as she is constantly checking her privilege and position within Black feminist spaces. Our collective offers an example of cross-race alliance, not only in the production of this work, but also the relationships and support we've provided to one another over the years. Here, we will explore the meaning of sisterhood within Black and white feminisms and consider how, historically, cross-race alliances among women have been formed through mutual struggle and intersectional approaches to liberation. As a collective, we believe that Olivia's unique position allows her to examine white feminism as both an insider (white woman) and outsider (practitioner of Black feminism and critical of white feminism). In the second part of the chapter, we collectively discuss accountability, what it looks like and what is needed to ensure mutual liberation, especially within academic settings.

The Meaning of Sisterhood through Olivia's Eyes

This likely goes without saying: definitions of sisterhood are culturally bound and group specific. Indeed, while the definitions of sisterhood as envisioned by Black and white women specifically are considered here, the concept of sisterhood has also been taken up by Chicana feminists, mestiza and Tejana feminists, Native American feminists, and a long list of additional multiracial and multicultural feminist perspectives not mentioned here. As a white woman, however, I will stay in my lane and focus on what I know best: understandings of sisterhood between and within Black and white feminist spaces.

In white women's spaces, sisterhood is typically used as a rallying cry to motivate unity in white feminist movement. In Bonnie Thornton Dill's (1983) "Prospects for an All-Inclusive Sisterhood" she describes this version of sisterhood as the anvil upon which we white women forge our political identities. Any white woman who came to feminism as a consequence of suddenly becoming aware of the limitations of her agency is probably familiar with this conceptualization of sisterhood. In white feminist spaces the call to sisterhood is a call that, when invoked, likely produces feelings of attachment to other women and a sense of duty to "the cause." Speaking from my own experience, this rings true.

I initially came to think of sisterhood as the tool white women would use to achieve liberation, but I also came to understand it as a weapon we could use against other feminists who "fell out of line." I have a vivid memory of criticizing some white politician in a women's and gender studies class as an undergraduate and being met with resistance from one of my peers who responded with something to the effect of, "I get what she said was problematic but we're all women. They want us to turn against each other and to attack each other and that's why we can never get anything done. We should really be focused on the men." The nods from our peers convinced me: among white women, good feminists don't criticize other women.

This version of sisterhood has been criticized by Black feminists for as long as white women have invoked its call. Black feminists see it for what it is: a strategic obscuring of the power dynamics that exist among women. When white feminists have invoked "universal sisterhood" it has been in an effort to *dismiss* the significance of racism, classism, and other systems of power that differentially impact women. This, of course, conveniently ensures that the problems stemming from sexism alone receive priority. This is why calls to sisterhood are often coupled with statements like "all women are oppressed" or "we might come from different backgrounds but we are the same in our experience with sexism!" These statements suggest that no matter how different we are, we share a common experience with oppression. We don't.

Black women's conceptualizations of sisterhood are not so limited. Research on this topic, for instance, reveals that its uses are wider and more varied than for white women (Joseph, 1981; hooks, 1984; Fox-Genovese, 1991). While sisterhood language does appear in Black women's political organizing—as in the late 19th century Black women's club movement discussed in Chapter 2—its relevance is not specific to traditional notions of politics. For example, sisterhood is thought of as a formal collective in some Black churches where becoming a "Sister" is a rite of passage that marks a woman as a full member of the church (Thornton Dill, 1983). The concept is additionally meaningful in fictive and extended kinship structures where sisterhood networks provide stability and mutual support for communities (Joseph, 1981). Sisterhood, for Black women, thus seems to be a thing that is nurtured (as in family structures), strived for (in community), and attended to (in political organizing) (Joseph, 1981; hooks, 1984; Fox-Genovese, 1991; Thornton Dill, 1983).

Even in the club movement of the 19th century, sisterhood was fostered through the process of working in community with other women who shared a purpose, not upon the assumption of sameness in experience (Davis, 1983). This is not my experience with white feminism. While I cannot say that all white women share my experience with feminism, at the very least I am comfortable saying that many white feminists do not understand sisterhood as something we must struggle toward, nurture, and cultivate. As history shows, white women tend to treat sisterhood as a given—a consequence of coincidence where allegiance is assured, not earned, by virtue of our womanhood. Therein lies one of the greatest barriers to cross-race sisterhood.

The barriers to sisterhood across race and class lines run deep. Historically, the relationship between Black and white women has by and large been one of exploitation and oppression. This is true within and without feminism. In her examination of Black and white women's relations in the antebellum south, Elizabeth Fox-Genovese (1988) dismisses the frankly asinine suggestion made by Clinton (1982) that white women and Black women experienced a form of sisterly solidarity in their shared experience as the "property" of white men. This is, obviously, an incredibly reductive retelling of history. White women were not passive bystanders who participated in slavery only to the extent that we happened to reside in our husband's labor camps. We actively participated in the slavery economy. As Jones-Rogers (2019) illustrates in *They Were Her Property*, white women bought and sold enslaved people, attended auctions, and subsequently lobbied for compensation after emancipation claiming "loss of human property."

Even in spaces where white women came together with freed Black women, the power dynamics between the two were never acknowledged in a way that would have been required for sisterly solidarity. In fact, those power dynamics were specifically weaponized. While white women played an important role in abolition societies, they would ultimately co-opt what they learned in these spaces for their own gain. In the "Declaration of Sentiments (1848)," or what many white women consider the founding document of the U.S. women's suffrage movement—Elizabeth Cady Stanton and the other all-white authors and signatories (with the exception of Frederick Douglass) leave the issue of slavery wholly unaddressed (Stanton & Douglass, 2011). While Black women suffered under the systems of chattel slavery, white women at the Seneca Falls Convention identified property rights, marriage, and the right to pursue work outside of the home as the principal problems facing women.

Tensions between white abolitionists and suffragists eventually came to a head over questions about literacy and Black male suffrage. This resulted in a schism within suffrage organizing because some whites supported Black male suffrage while others did not, claiming "women's equality" was of greater importance. Susan B. Anthony and Elizabeth Cady Stanton were the most prominent leaders of this newly formed latter group known as the National Woman Suffrage Association (NWSA). On frequent occasions in Anthony's capacity as leader of the NWSA she resorted to white supremacist language in her rhetoric on the importance of securing the vote for *white* women. Following the passage of the 15th Amendment, suffragists united once again under the founding of the National American Women's Suffrage Association (NAWSA) in 1890 This organization attempted to achieve suffrage by securing it at the state level in enough states such that congress would eventually be forced to pass a federal amendment. Eventually, however, the southern chapters of the NAWSA would oppose efforts to secure a federal amendment knowing that such an achievement would more than likely result in the enfranchisement of Black women. Abandoned by their white "sisters," Black women did not effectively obtain the vote until the Voting Rights Act of 1965 (Jones, 2020).

As the suffrage movement began gaining speed in the late 19th and early 20th centuries, so too did the women's temperance movement, spearheaded by Frances Willard and the Women's Christian Temperance Union, and the antilynching movement, led by a Black woman named Ida B. Wells. At nearly every turn, however, the Women's Christian Temperance Union (a group advocating for prohibition as a matter of women's rights) publicly undermined Wells' efforts. Frances Willard, for instance, implied that lynching was justified in response to the mythologized violence of Black men. She made this comment while preaching "sisterly bonds" with Black women, both in an effort to gain their support for prohibition and to dismiss Wells' criticism of their activities (Frances Willard House Museum Archives). Sisterhood language was also central to women's prison reform activism around the same time. White Christian reformer women used sisterhood in this context to exert control over incarcerated Black and poor women. Women who did not fit the feminine ideal—an ideal informed by white, middle-class gender norms—were excluded from becoming a "sister" and attending the women-only rehabilitation alternative to the more common co-ed incarceration facilities (Freedman, 1981; LeFlouria, 2015; Haley, 2016). Here again we see sisterhood as a means of not just exerting power over Black women but enforcing sameness among women.

The birth control movement in the early 20th century proved to be another space where white women were more than ready to sell out women of color when called upon to do so. In *Women, Race & Class*, Angela Davis argues that Margaret Sanger's early birth control campaign—which was born out of anti-poverty/pro-socialist organizing—had the potential to unite women across race and class lines. This, of course, did not happen. Sanger abandoned the anti-poverty agenda she originally viewed as so central to the birth control campaign and instead adopted a eugenics position advocating instead for population control of the "underclasses" (Davis, 1983). By the late 1930s, Sanger endorsed projects and organizations dedicated to restricting childbearing among communities of color through the use of propaganda and compulsory sterilization. Without any attention given to the racist history of reproductive rights and white women's role in weaponizing the birth control campaign, a few decades later women's liberationists would turn to Black women once again with their silver tongue pleas to join the cause in the name of sisterhood.

Although sister-language has been used by white feminists across the centuries, calls to a universal sisterhood by white feminists featured heavily during the Women's Liberation Movement of the 1960s and 1970s. This moment in feminism is generally associated with concern over the burdens of the "housewife"—what Betty Friedan (1963) refers to as "the problem with no name" or, the plight of suburban wives who felt unfulfilled, unhappy, and empty in their role as the homemaker. As the first president of the National Organization of Women (NOW), Friedan made the problem with no name the priority of the organization. Similar to their suffrage forebearers who crafted the Declaration of Sentiments in the image of the Declaration of Independence a little over a century earlier, NOW drafted a Bill of Rights for Women and codified the prioritization of white women. The concerns of Black women, poor women, Latina women, immigrant women, and lesbian women were not considered and this, of course, angered a significant portion of the group's membership. Friedan doubled-down arguing, "the gut issues of this revolution involve employment and education" (1963, p. 6). She justified this stance by insisting that the desire to obtain a career outside of the home and one's role as a wife and mother is a problem that all women share *as women*.

Feminists who mobilized around the predicament of the suburban housewife would call women of color to join their organizations in the name of sisterhood arguing that all women shared a common source of oppression—sexism. It was in this shared experience of oppression, Women's Liberationists argued, that the bonds of sisterhood would supposedly be forged. Yet, in making the predicament of the suburban housewife the focus of the movement and the foundation upon which sisterly solidarity could be built, white women not only sidelined Black women whose experiences with oppression could not be explained by sexism alone; they mythologized sisterly solidarity as something that could be born out of shared victimization, similarity, and uniformity. In *From Margin to Center* (1984) bell hooks criticizes this conceptualization of sisterhood for its reliance on patriarchal stereotypes about women as victims and its universalizing of women's experiences. This version of sisterhood asks Black women to deny the ways in which racism, among other systems of power, shape their experiences with oppression while allowing privileged white women to "abdicate responsibility" for their role as oppressors. Indeed, if white women could successfully position all women as "equally oppressed" there is no need to interrogate (and then dismantle) the systems that differentially privilege and oppress all women.

White feminists today continue to invoke sisterhood and sameness to ensure white women's problems remain centered in feminist activism. At the national level and in the local "sister marches," the 2017 Women's March on Washington (WMW) was dripping with references to sisterly solidarity as white feminists on the ground bemoaned the integration of an intersectional analysis of women's issues. The intersectional approach only came after mainly transwomen and women of color feminists criticized the organization for their all-white leadership and centering of white cis womanhood. In response, women of color and queer women were brought on as leaders and the WMW published a mission statement that was decidedly intersectional in nature (Stockman, 2017). Yet the change brought on another wave of criticism, this time from white women who could not understand why a march dedicated to "all women" was "making it about race." Facebook events and groups for local "sister marches" lit up with angry white women who insisted "we are all oppressed!" "Why can't we set aside our differences and focus on our similarities?" they wanted to know.

These themes came up in interviews I conducted for my dissertation (McLaughlin, 2020) nearly two years later. Stella (pseudonym), a middle-aged white woman who sees Friedan's "problem with no name" as the biggest issue facing women, could not understand why race was brought up at all. "It got really weird because it felt like they [Black women] wanted to make it more about race than feminism," she said (McLaughlin, forthcoming). It's worth noting here that Stella was not the lone participant convinced that race and racism were not pertinent issues for feminists. When I asked Rita (pseudonym), a 20-something white woman hoping to become a lawyer, if she thought race and racism were relevant in feminism, she became frustrated and flustered. "Feminism is—it's not what the definition is… It says nothing about race," she explained. She continued, "Feminism and racial equality are separate fights… If we're just talking about definitions here—'What is feminism?'—we're not talking about racism in that discussion…. I don't know. I'm just very confused about this question" (McLaughlin, 2020, p. 171). Participants like Stella and Rita could not imagine why it might be necessary to highlight differences among women rather than obscure them by focusing on sameness. Thus, it seems the barriers to sisterhood lie not only in the legacy of exploitation and violence within white feminism but also in our continued insistence that sameness among women is the foundation upon which sisterly solidarity is built.

The Blueprint: A Model Does Exist

While I was not all too surprised to encounter some resistance to intersectional feminism when conducting research for my dissertation, I was surprised to find the vast majority of participants readily acknowledged the significance of white privilege. Assuming that white feminist's problem was our denial of the significance of whiteness, I viewed race awareness as *the thing* that might bring about sisterhood. While the feminists I interviewed did not explicitly deny their racial privilege, they did not think of racism as a problem relevant to white women. For them, issues related to race fell at the feet of women of color. When Lilly (pseudonym) shared a story about witnessing discrimination against a Black woman she works with, I asked her how she reacted to the incident and if she and her coworker ever spoke about it. Lilly explained she did not know how to react and never spoke about it with her coworker. I asked her why and she said, "I don't know. I don't have that kind of relationship with her. Plus, it scares me to talk about race with her because I'm [expletive] white! Like, I don't know. It feels inappropriate, like it's not my business" (McLaughlin, 2020, p. 152). *Inappropriate. Not my business.*

Thanks to Black feminist historians, white women do not have to look far to identify models for sisterhood. I will explore some of these models below, but it is important to note the purpose of such an exploration. While white women do not necessarily need to be lifted up more than we already are in feminist history, we cannot continue co-opting and appropriating Black women's contributions and history and pretend this makes us "good" feminists. In her piece on the "second wave" of feminism, Becky Thompson writes, "White women, look to your own history for signs of heresy and rebellion" (2002, p. 63). Because white supremacy demands white solidarity, heresy and rebellion by white women necessarily involves cross-race solidarity. For this reason, I challenge every white woman who has marched with a quote from a Black feminist on their protest sign or invoked the call to sisterhood to explore the history of cross-race solidarity among women. Doing so reveals that racism *is* our business. Working together, Black women and *some* white women have made racism their business, not in an effort to "save" or "help" but in recognition that white women will never be free so long as Black women are oppressed.

When looking to history for examples of Black and white women working together in sisterly solidarity, the few examples we do have feature white women with an acute understanding of the intersecting nature of oppression.

They knew that the oppression of Black women was not unrelated to their own. They nurtured sisterly solidarity in hopes of achieving mutual liberation. The Grimke Sisters provide one of the most powerful examples of sisterly solidarity formed on the basis of mutual liberation. Sarah and Angelina Grimke, both abolitionists and proponents of women's rights, challenged their contemporaries to acknowledge the bond linking white women with enslaved Black women: "They are our country women—*they are our sisters;* and to us, as women, they have a right to look for sympathy with their sorrows, and effort and prayer for their rescue" (in Davis, 1983, p. 44, original emphasis).

What makes the Grimkes so noteworthy is their clear awareness of the intersecting nature of oppression and the entanglement of systems of power. In chronicling the history of women's activism at the intersection of race and class, Angela Davis argues that the Grimke Sisters avoided the "ideological snare" women like Susan B. Anthony and Elizabeth Cady Stanton were caught in. Unlike Anthony and Stanton who (as we have discussed elsewhere in this book) viewed women's oppression as an issue altogether separate from Black liberation, the Grimkes saw Black liberation and women's liberation as *dialectical* in nature. In simple terms, they understood that the oppression of white women was connected to the oppression of Black women. They understood how white supremacy and patriarchy worked together to maintain oppression and, as a result, knew that white women would necessarily benefit from a movement that prioritized the needs of the Black women. It is also worth noting: Unlike Susan B. Anthony and other white women who deployed "the metaphor of slavery" to describe their condition under patriarchy, the Grimke Sisters never compared marriage to slavery. Always a plus.

As an educator, I also find Prudence Crandall particularly compelling, not just because of her belief in the importance of education for African Americans. As school teachers, many Black women and men established schools in the early 19th century, despite the many laws that prohibited teaching enslaved and even free Blacks how to read and write (Hamilton, 2024). As a white woman, Crandall stands out, however, because she was ready to put her body and safety on the line. Originally hailing from Connecticut, she was militant in her convictions and rejected white solidarity with the people in her town by educating Black girls and women, even at the risk of her life. Crandall was not the only person championing Black education rights in the early 19th century. The lack of education for women and girls is mentioned in the Declaration of Sentiments by its white feminist framers. Almost two decades prior, however, Maria W. Stewart, a Black woman born free, made education a primary concern in her public lectures and writings (Guy-Sheftall, 1995). Stewart was the first woman of any race to give a public lecture in the United States and in 1831 published a piece in the abolitionist pamphlet *The Liberator*. Her essay called for women to unite under the cause of education for Black girls and women:

> ...[L]et us make a mighty effort and arise, let every female heart become united, and let us raise a fund ourselves; and at the end of one year and a half, we might be able to lay the cornerstone for the building of a high school, that the higher branches of knowledge might be enjoyed by us... How long shall the fair daughters of Africa be compelled to bury their minds and talents beneath a load of iron pots and kettles? Until union, knowledge and love begin to flow among us.

While Crandall never spoke publicly about Stewart and there is no indication they ever met, because of Crandall's upbringing and relationships with abolitionist organizers, she likely read Stewart's essay in *The Liberator* (Rycenga, 2005). Prudence Crandall responded to the call and opened her school to Black girls two years later. Originally, Crandall intended to teach Black and white children alike. It was only after the white parents removed their daughters from the institute that she decided to change the school into an institute for Black girls exclusively (Davis, 1983).

Outraged, the townspeople refused to sell Crandall materials and doctors would not provide medical care to the children (Davis, 1983). Numerous lawsuits were filed against her in hopes of forcing her to close the school. She would not relent. In response, the townspeople rioted and set fire to her schoolhouse multiple times (Davis, 1983). On Crandall, Angela Davis writes "Lucidly and eloquently, her actions spoke of the vast possibilities for liberation if white women en masse would join hands with their Black sisters" (1983, p. 26). The school was open for a little over a year but in the time it operated the young women and girls who came together demonstrated immense bravery. They defied vigilante violence, persisted amidst lawsuits, and realized a shared goal through mutual struggle. Although the school was forced to close after Crandall's arrest, a number of the students went on to become teachers themselves (Rycenga, 2005). Margaret Douglass, one of Crandall's contemporaries, similarly opened a school where she and her daughter taught Black children how to read (Davis, 1983). She was charged and arrested for violating Virginia law stating that Black people could not congregate to read and write. Unable to afford an attorney for her trial, she was found guilty and incarcerated.

While the Grimke Sisters, Crandall, and Douglass are commendable in their own right, some of the most powerful examples of white women's solidarity with Black liberation come from communist and socialist feminism in the late 19th and early 20th century. These women are different from those discussed above in that they tended to speak more directly to white people about whiteness (Davis, 1983). Anita Whitney, for instance, did not shy away from calling out her white sisters when addressing the problem of lynching. At a time when the myth about the Black rapist was nearly ubiquitous in white feminist organizing (as I describe above it was used to motivate support for not just white women's suffrage but prohibition as well), Whitney kept a clear head (Davis, 1983). She remained vigilant, relying on statistics and reason as a source of truth rather than white supremacist propaganda. The following comes from a speech Anita Whitney gave to a white women's club:

> Since 1890, when our statistics have their beginning, there have occurred in these United States 3,228 lynchings… I would that I could leave the subject with these bare facts…but I feel we must face all the barbarity of the situation in order to do our part in blotting this disgrace from our country's record… Do you wonder…that a colored man once said that if he owned Hell and Texas he would prefer to rent out Texas and live in Hell, for he had these supporting facts that…since 1890 Texas had lynched 338 human beings, second only to Georgia and Mississippi in this horrible eminence? (in Davis, 1983, p. 160).

When she stepped down from the stage after giving her speech, she was arrested.

Ella Reeve Bloor (known as "Mother Bloor") was another white communist woman who realized the necessity of Black liberation through the working-class struggle. She demonstrated, unlike Betty Freidan, another labor organizer, the necessity of working across both class and racial lines. Mother Bloor, a pacifist, trade union organizer and member of the socialist and eventually the communist party, was born in 1862. Her autobiography (see Bloor, 1940) depicts a militant and thoughtful activist who aligned with workers across multiple industries, protested the exploitation of immigrants, and fought against the inhumane incarceration conditions of the early 20th century. In describing Mother Bloor as an antiracist, Angela Davis points out that while her socialist and "working-class consciousness did not include an explicit awareness of Black people's special oppression" (1983, p. 155), her work later in life, as a member of the communist party, demonstrates a fervent commitment to anti-racism. Indeed, Bloor writes in her autobiography of the inspiration she drew from her ancestors' staunch commitment to Black liberation in spite of the personal consequences:

> I am proud of the fact that some of my ancestors on my mother's side were pioneers of the anti-slavery movement....But there were also Tories among my ancestors who tried to disown their more revolutionary relatives, and for that reason I never discovered until I was sixty years old the most distinguished of all my ancestors, for his name was never mentioned in the family.... Thaddeus Stevens, that great fighter for human freedom was an uncompromising abolitionist... His championship of social as well as political equality for Negores was the real reason for the family's disapproval of him (1940, p. 18).

Bloor drew inspiration from her cousin's commitment—so strong it resulted in his estrangement from the family—and found in him, as we can find in her, strength to defy the strongholds of white solidarity.

In her work as an organizer, Bloor opposed the segregation of the Black delegates from the International Labor Defense convention and other labor rights events and seemed to have played an active role in ensuring Black women's presence at conferences and conventions (Davis, 1983). She spoke out publicly against lynching, addressing whites directly, and spoke of the importance of ending "the imperialism of the United States in all its manifestations" (1940, p. 185) by supporting "complete legal, economic, and social equality" for Black people.

Like Crandall, Ella Reeve Bloor did not relent when the going got tough. In her autobiography (1940) she claims to have been arrested "hundreds of times" and indeed she was no stranger to incarceration. Around 1936, Mother Bloor traveled to Nebraska to meet with farmers and network with other organizers in hopes of gaining support for an anti-war conference. While in Nebraska, Bloor and Mrs. Floyd Booth (referred to as her married name in all accounts)—a Black woman whose role as secretary of the anti-war committee overlapped with Bloor—attended a meeting in support of women striking against the inhumane working conditions on a poultry farm. In Bloor's autobiography, she recalls how the meeting was "set upon by a crowd of thugs... armed with blackjacks and with deadly weapons" (p. 251). Mrs. Booth's husband—an organizer himself—was pursued by the crowd as they yelled racial slurs. Although Mrs. Booth and her husband were not seriously injured, they (along with Mother Bloor) were arrested and held in jail for nearly two weeks. To secure bail for Bloor, some socialist farmers raised funds for her release but she refused to leave if the Floyd Booths could not accompany her:

[A] good old Socialist farmer was ready to put up bail for me. I asked him if there was bail for Floyd Booth and his wife, too, and they told me the farmers were too poor... I could not accept the bail and leave the two Negro comrades in jail, in an atmosphere so dangerously charged with bitter hate of Negroes (1940, p. 252).

Eleven days into their incarceration, the Booths were released. Only then did Mother Bloor attempt to secure her own release.

In what remained of her life, Mother Bloor allied again and again with Black liberation through her pro-labor activism. She organized on behalf of sharecroppers, Black women workers, and immigrant rights. She believed that a working-class movement could not be successful if it did not "struggle relentlessly against the social poison of racism" (Davis, 1983, p. 93). For white feminists today, Mother Bloor illustrates the importance of moving beyond such a limited understanding of "women's issues." Thornton Dill (1983) argues as much in "Prospects for an All-Inclusive Sisterhood" when she urges women to consider ways to align with groups that address aspects of oppression beyond those we typically associate with feminism (i.e., white women's problems). This, of course, requires white women to move into spaces of social justice outside of those we commonly regard as "feminist" (e.g., abortion, violence against women).

Black Feminism, the Path Forward

As I discussed in Chapter 6, I have come to adopt the perspective of my mentor, Dr. Richardson: Black feminism can be thought of as a liberation handbook for white women. This was a groundbreaking idea for me, since I had always thought of Black feminism as one of many "third wave" feminisms located at the back of the feminist theory book and "not meant for me." Fortunately, my study of cross-race solidarity in feminism has revealed that Dr. Richardson's perspective is part of the tradition of Black feminism. Maria W. Stewart invoked the call for sisterly solidarity, one that Crandall answered. In 1861, Sojourner Truth made a similar plea. Truth was born into slavery but became a freed woman in 1826 (Guy-Sheftall, 1995). She is most well known for her "Ain't I a Woman?" speech—one of the earliest examples of intersectional theorizing in American feminism—but in her lesser known speech "When Woman Gets Her Rights Man Will be Right," Truth illustrates her understanding of the bound fates of Black and white women as well as the relationship between race, gender, and class oppression:

> There is a great stir about colored men getting their rights, but not a word about the colored women'... They go out washing, which is about as high as a colored woman gets, and their men go about idle, strutting up and down... I want women to have their rights. In the courts women have no right, no voice... I have done a great deal of work–as much as a man, but did not get so much pay. I used to work in the field and bind grain... but men never doing no more, got twice as much pay. So with the German women. They work in the field and do as much work, but do not get the pay. We do as much, but do not get the pay.

Truth aligns herself here with poor German women but throughout the speech she references the liberation of women as a whole—including wealthier white women—while advocating for the centering of Black women's needs *specifically*. Truth uses "we" and "our" in speaking about women but never essentializes us as a group—pointing out important differences in our conditions—and ends by advocating for the prioritization of Black women's suffrage. Truth, then, seems to have understood that the path to liberation was one that required women's mutual struggle toward improving the condition of the most marginalized. However, like Crenshaw's intersectionality has been co-opted in name and word only, Nell Painter (1997) demands we acknowledge the ways in which white feminists co-opted Truth's message.

The fact that Black women such as Truth and Stewart spoke and wrote about solidarity with white women demonstrates that cross-race alliances have existed and are possible. That *some* white women responded to the call demonstrates that many of us have not lived up to the bar set by our foremothers. If the stories above demonstrate anything, it is that real cross-race solidarity—the kind needed for sisterhood to manifest—is a struggle. Discourse on sisterhood in popular culture and in white feminist spaces does a disservice to liberation projects but also to white feminists who truly seek sisterly solidarity.

When I come across sisterhood in "the real world" I often think to myself, "whoever came up with this has never had a sister." Consider a few of my "favorites": "being sisters means you always have back up", "sisters are like fat thighs—they stick together", and "be the sister that straightens another woman's crown without telling the world it was crooked." These are superficial representations of sister relationships. They simultaneously suppress and sugarcoat the more nuanced relationship dynamics that typically exist among sisters, dynamics that can be painful in their complexity. They imply that sisterhood is a relationship free from strife, conflict, and struggle. Sometimes we cannot and should not provide unquestioning support to other women. Sometimes we should "straighten another woman's crown" in a public setting.

It is crucial to acknowledge the deep damage done by white women to Black women that causes Black women not to trust us. Our eagerness to weaponize victimhood and our tendency to lash out when confronted with evidence of our racism makes us untrustworthy and doubtful allies. Our strategic, weaponized use of tears as a mechanism of avoiding accountability is well-documented (see Cooper, 2018) and prevents sisterly solidarity based on mutual respect. True sisters should be able to endure conflict and healthy relationships necessitate criticism. Moreover, our treatment of one another is enough to make any woman of color skeptical of investing in a friendship with a white woman. In *White Women: Everything You Already Know About Your Own Racism* (2022), authors Regina Jackson and Saira Rao question how we can exist in true sisterhood with women of color when we cannot even achieve sisterhood among ourselves? White women's friendships, they write, are characterized by back-stabbing, gossip, constant competition, and saccharine niceties rather than genuine kindness. For Jackson and Rao, cross-race sisterhood is only possible if we can exist in community with one another first. Absent this intraracial work, we risk replicating toxicity in a relationship dynamic that is vastly more complex and nuanced given the power dynamics between white women and women of Color.

As white feminists attempt to transform their relationship with white supremacy and with Black women, we cannot be surprised when we are questioned by those we attempt to align with. Here the deep distrust that Black women held (and still hold) for white women (and for good reason), complicates these seeming instances of solidarity (see hooks, 1984; Cooper, 2018). These factors make sisterhood and solidarity a substantially complex notion; it is in no way simple.

The purpose of outlining the history of exploitation and oppression between Black and white women at the start of this chapter is to make absolutely clear that we should not expect a "clean slate". We should expect to be challenged and we deserve nothing less than to be put to the test. Real sisters do not stop speaking to one another or vow to never again show up to the family reunion after one tells the other, they are being selfish. Real sisters fight and good sisters know that the best apology is changed behavior. White women: we have been selfish. Cry about it, if you want, but do it in private. And most importantly, listen to, read, believe, and cite Black women. McKenzie (2015) clearly spells out what white feminists must do:

When we talk about feminism and "inclusion" we need to remember that feminism doesn't belong to white women by default. **There is no feminism without women of color...** A next-level feminism, a game-changing feminism, is a feminism that *centers* women of color....Because white women benefit from the work that women of color do in pursuit of freedom and equality, they really ought to do a better job of being worthy of women of color and the work [Black women] do for women. When someone else's struggles benefit you, it behooves you to make those struggles easier, not more difficult...So, instead of asking "how can white women include women of color in feminism" we ought to be asking "when will white women make themselves worthy of the benefits they reap from the work of feminists of color?"

"Karens" express a dangerous kind of white supremacy, and if white feminists within the academy are not working toward being antiracist, they are dangerous and should be held accountable (Armstrong, 2021; Williams, 2020).

Accountability: White Folks, Getting Our People in Academic Spaces

Black women are underrepresented in faculty positions (Kazmi et al., 2022). For this reason, discussions about systemic inequality in higher education often focus on the need to increase the number of Black instructors and researchers hired for tenured and tenure-track positions (Durodoye et al., 2020; Rideau, 2021). This is important. Black students benefit from seeing themselves represented in the ranks of faculty positions (Croom & Patton, 2011) and white students need to see Black women in positions of authority and mastery. It is equally important, however, that white faculty and administrators examine the ways in which we make academia inhospitable to the Black people we already work with. Of course, this is not an original idea. Following a department meeting focused on ways to increase retention of Black students and diversity among the faculty in our graduate program, Keiondra expressed her frustration with such an approach. Over some sangrias and nachos at our local spot, Keiondra's take on the meeting went something like this: "White people always want to bring *more* Black people into a space they already know is toxic to us. Why subject more people to this hell hole before trying to make it better for those of us who are already here?" She's not wrong.

Black women in academia are put through it by their non-Black colleagues *and* their students. Demanding new lines for faculty while ignoring the slow violence that makes academia an inhospitable and downright toxic space for Black women is irresponsible and unproductive. We should all be wary of those who make loud requests for increasing faculty diversity while behaving in ways that directly and indirectly harm Black women. Hamilton (2020, p. 1) makes clear that "institutional racism has just as much of a nefarious impact on Black lives as any kind, and, if the administrators and leaders of these schools want us to take seriously their anti-racist commitments, then they need to acknowledge the undue harm that these institutions continue to inflict on their scarcely diverse communities." Without a consistent anti-racist practice, these folks are just petitioning to bring in more Black women they can torment. So, in addition to increasing the number of tenured and tenure-track Black faculty in our colleges and universities, white faculty must commit (in a long-term and tangible way) to intersectional, anti-racist practice and—importantly—this commitment needs to be supported and reinforced by university administration.

As white professors, there are specific steps we can take to ensure accountability. First, we need to petition and demand our universities hire outside evaluators to examine how racism and sexism manifests on our campuses. As the chief diversity officer for State University of New York at Buffalo's Graduate School of Education, Raechele Pope discussed the importance of these kinds of consultations in *Inside Higher Ed* (see Flaherty, 2020). These evaluations need to take place at the departmental, college, and university level. As Bell et al. (2021) demonstrate, some Black women are targeted by their chairs, others by their deans, and others still by university administrators. Some receive support from one level while being downright sabotaged at another, leading to a kind of bureaucratic whiplash. A comprehensive evaluation will demonstrate how these levels interact in ways that advance, mitigate, and/or reinforce the targeting of Black academic women. Clinical sociologists and institutional ethnographers are specifically trained for this kind of work, so let's make use of them.

Following these evaluations, we need to urge universities to employ and establish long-term relationships with third-party consultants who will work with white faculty and staff to address the evaluation's findings. These consultations must go beyond the "diversity, equity, and inclusion"-style workshops we are all familiar with. As an assistant professor, I know the majority of my colleagues (both on my campus and elsewhere) view these workshops as trite and a waste of time. I too find them largely unhelpful. In my experience diversity, equity, and inclusion workshops tend to discuss oppression in unspecific, hypothetical, and banal terms. They suggest, "everyone experiences some form of oppression!" As the current push against Critical Race Theory and "divisive concepts" illustrates, they do this likely in hopes of creating a space that feels unthreatening to very privileged people, who tend to make up the majority of attendees. Additionally, I have yet to attend a university-sponsored diversity and inclusion workshop that goes beyond merely asking folks to name and reflect on their privileges. To be clear, the ability to recognize one's privilege is the floor, not the ceiling. Moreover, any approach to anti-racism and anti-sexism that attempts to create a comfortable space for oppressors will not help Black women. Systems of inequality are inherently threatening with consequences that are both tangible and specific.

As an alternative, we need educational workshops in addition to trained consultants—*not* unpaid Black faculty and staff—who will discuss the specific problematic behaviors and practices with those responsible. As Raechele Pope (see Flaherty, 2020) argues, if Black faculty want to participate in these evaluations and consultations they must be paid for their work and their labor needs to be counted as progress toward tenure and promotion. In the meantime, co-conspirators should not stop attending these workshops. We should maintain a presence in these spaces to ensure conversations about power and inequity are not sterilized.

In addition to this institutional-level work, white professors need to organize across departments to help one another make anti-racism, anti-sexism, and intersectional analyses of power a habit. Race is an inherently social project (Bonilla-Silva, 2018). As a result, anti-racism cannot be done in isolation. Our commitment to anti-racist practice must go beyond "book clubs." I have participated in several and, while they are a start, the conversations tend to be overly theoretical and participants shy away from viewing themselves as racists, as illustrated in my experience with the *Eloquent Rage* book club. Put simply, in the same way reading about brain surgery does not make one a brain surgeon, reading about anti-racism does not make one an anti-racist.

As white academics, we need to caucus and identify the ways in which we reinforce racism and sexism. Once we understand *how* we uphold patriarchal and white supremacy on our campuses, we can work together to abolish our harmful policies and practices. This includes the harmful policies and practices in our teaching that disproportionately target Black students. Our Black colleagues must not be required to participate in these sessions (or any session devoted to anti-racism). If they wish to participate, they must be paid for their work and their labor needs to be counted as progress toward tenure and promotion.

CONCLUSION

Administrative Accountability

As we revise these chapters, months before going to press, significant changes and events have transpired in relation to the narratives and experiences we've shared. After Jennifer and Mariam submitted their 2020 OIE complaint, Jennifer submitted a second OIE complaint in 2022 in response to her denial for early tenure at the Dean and interim Provost level. As a result of this denial, Jennifer submitted new evidence of the Dean's tenure decision requiring extracontractual conditions to be met before Jennifer could receive tenure (including specific number and types of publications and continuing to discourage her service work). From Jennifer's observation, this appeared to be retaliation for her initial 2020 complaints and for Jennifer's criticism regarding the Dean. As part of the 2022 complaint, Jennifer submitted an email thread (where she was boldly critical of the Dean) with the previous Provost who was instrumental in Mariam, Jennifer, and Staci's transfer out of GWS. This email thread was then accidentally shared with the Dean. After a series of appeals and meetings, the recommendation for Jennifer's early tenure was finally denied by the interim Provost, with modified conditions.

Literally, five minutes after Jennifer received the final positive with revised conditions report (aligned with the Dean's initial denial) from the office of the interim Provost, Mariam, Staci, and Jennifer received emails from the interim Provost that suddenly attended to concerns about the GWS department:

> Concerns have been raised by multiple individuals, including faculty and staff, regarding the current environment and direction of the Department of Gender and Women's Studies. After careful consideration, I have determined that the best course of action is to bring in a disinterested third party to conduct an inquiry, including one-on-one interviews with members of the department, to help me better understand the issues behind the articulated concerns, specific problems that need to be addressed, and the root cause(s) for the alleged issues regarding shared governance and other reported issues within this unit. To accomplish this, the services of [Mr. Tan] have been retained [website linked showing an African American attorney well versed in corporate and employment law provided]
>
> [Mr. Tan] will be reaching out to you directly to schedule an appointment. I would like to thank you in advance for meeting with him to provide your insights.

Although these concerns were raised by the majority of GWS faculty in 2017–2020 and again during Jennifer's early promotion review and appeals in 2022, suddenly the interim Provost was interested in investigating problems and complaints about the GWS department. Despite OIE's charge for investigating Jennifer and Mariam's formal complaints, this strategy appeared to be more about protecting administration and the university than resolving departmental issues and concerns. In fact, OIE responded to Jennifer's 2022 complaint (interviewing only Jennifer as faculty) saying that they found no evidence to suggest retaliation or discrimination on the part of the Dean nor interim Provost. Ultimately, we learned that two of the remaining four faculty made their complaints known about M. Ann and Karen. This of course left us feeling like the concerns of Black women did not initiate such an inquiry but instead, white women in the department who were vying for power and tipping the scale. Mariam, Staci, and Becca met with Mr. Tan to recount the historical abuse and toxicity within the department and the harms caused by the Dean, M. Ann, and Karen. Jennifer opted not to meet with Mr. Tan and instead asked that he review her hundreds of pages of the OIE complaints and even this book manuscript. We never received a follow-up meeting or report about the outcome of this meeting or investigation.

Despite the fact that the formal findings from the interim Provost's investigation were not shared with any of us who first initiated the complaint, a press release concerning the decision to close the GWS department was suddenly sent by the Dean, Interim Provost and an Associate Dean of CAS college wide:

Gender and Women's Studies Update

Sept. 16, 2022

The Gender and Women's Studies faculty, courses and programs have long provided critically important content and educational opportunities for WMU's students and the broader community. This will continue to be the case as Gender and Women's Studies (GWS) undergoes a future administrative restructuring in which it will cease to be a stand-alone department with a chair but will otherwise remain unchanged. With this development, GWS will continue as a major and minor, and it will continue to provide the strong curriculum and courses it has always offered. The structural modification is administrative only.

No faculty, part-time instructor or staff lines will be eliminated under the restructuring. We will continue to provide students with access to GWS programs and courses, which will continue to be taught by outstanding faculty and part-time instructors.

WMU first established an interdisciplinary Women's Studies program in the 1970s, which was broadened to a Gender and Women's Studies program in 2007. Faculty from a wide variety of academic units have contributed their scholarly expertise and courses to these programs for decades.

In 2013, the Faculty Senate recommended, and the Board of Trustees approved, a proposal to replace the interdisciplinary Gender and Women's Studies program with a Department of Gender and Women's Studies. This change was recommended in recognition that the program had grown to include five Board-approved faculty appointments, with 54 students majoring and 48 students minoring in Gender and Women's Studies.

Since that time, national searches in 2015 and 2019 resulted in the hires of two faculty with primary appointments in GWS, and two faculty members transferred their primary appointment into GWS from another academic unit in the college. However, of the total nine faculty who have held primary faculty appointments in GWS since it became a department in 2013, seven have subsequently requested that the administration transfer them out of the unit, with only two remaining. Five of these transfers have been granted and approved by the Board of Trustees, and two current requests are in process. In addition, among students, the number of Gender and Women's Studies majors has declined to 12 as of fall 2022, and the number of student credit hours (SCH) has steadily declined from 7,039 SCH in 2012–2013 to 2,616 SCH in 2021–2022.

With current faculty requests for immediate, permanent transfer out of GWS and only two faculty lines remaining in the unit, the rationale articulated in 2013 for a stand-alone Gender and Women's Studies Department has been significantly diminished. CAS is cognizant of concerns that have been articulated regarding efficient investment in administrative overhead. Therefore, while fully retaining the program, the college intends to eliminate the department, and to work with faculty with relevant content expertise from across the university to move the Gender and Women's Studies major, minor and courses to another existing academic unit for administrative purposes.

With these coming changes, we remain committed to continuing to support these important interdisciplinary programs so that they may thrive and grow at WMU.

This announcement felt like a full circle moment, with the reinstatement of AAAS, and karmic evidence that when power is built on a shaky foundation of white supremacy it doesn't last; social justice and equity do. However, we also cannot overstate that full accountability is not in the closing of the department. We believe that the institution manipulated, maneuvered, and took advantage of us to serve their own purposes in closing the department. They did not care about the legacy of harm that M. Ann and Karen caused until it impacted white women, Rachel, Becca and the interim chair that served in Becca's leave of absence as chair. The Dean could no longer make excuses for them as enrollment was low and there were now no longer enough faculty willing to stay in the department.

As it comes to accountability, this latest ordeal between GWS, the Dean, and now the union (led by AAUP president, M. Ann) is, at this moment, very much unresolved, and the irony is not lost on us. Currently, at the time of this writing, there is an intense dispute between the Dean and AAUP about closing the GWS department. Mariam's story, previously shared, highlights the demise of the Africana Studies program, which M. Ann worked to dismantle. Her story also highlights the lack of intervention on behalf of the union to dispute the closing of the program. Some suggested that this was because Africana Studies was not really a department; however, program closures are covered under shared governance principles and impact bargaining that could have happened had the union cared enough for Black studies to take up the cause.

At the end of the day, closing the department is not true vindication for us. Additionally, the Dean, who still has escaped full accountability, maintains authority over us. It is bittersweet: the exculpation of evidence of the harm done simultaneously reveals more of the same sleights of hand tricks this administration is up to by protecting themselves and using institutional vendettas to retaliate. In fact, we are already planning on a follow up article to continue telling our truths; recording our accounts of anticipated or realized backlash; and the outcomes of the accountability and potential reconciliation on the part of administrators.

While we have started the coup, and progressed toward an escape from some of the agents of white supremacist feminists, we know that systemic and liberatory change must be possible. But we cannot overstate the requirement to continue to fight for accountability and justice in the telling of our stories and the naming of injustice. In what follows, we provide additional action steps toward institutional change that should be taken as a precaution so as to avoid *some* of the mess academic institutions create for Black women and marginalized people.

Action Step 1: Elevate the Weight of Service as Qualifications for Tenure

A large body of literature exists on the "service tax" that Black women pay with respect to tenure and promotion (Arnold et al., 2021; Baker-Bell, 2020; Griffin et al., 2013). More precisely, given the underrepresentation of Black women in the academy, they often get called upon to serve on diversity and inclusion-related committees, theses and dissertations about race, and are called upon to mentor multiple BIPOC students because they are often the only faculty who share a collective set of experiences with these students.

Just recently, Jennifer submitted her file for tenure and promotion review, where the Dean chastised her scholarly productivity due to her service commitments, noting:

> As detailed in her [tenure file], Dr. Richardson has been frequently called upon to provide a great deal of 'invisible service' and mentorship, especially to BIPOC students. I am deeply appreciative to Dr. Richardson for her unwavering support of student success... I strongly caution Dr. Richardson not to take on too much service; I recommend that she reduces [sic] her current service commitments so that she has more time to focus on her [research and scholarship] activities.

From Jennifer's perspective, however, she extended her service to the University and College's mission of Diversity, Equity and Inclusion. Many times, her unique professional recognition, scholarship and identity as a Black woman, positions her as the only or one of a few faculty members capable of the requested service (especially in the College of Arts and Sciences [CAS]). It is also important to note, while she is called upon to mentor BIPOC students, especially due to such a dearth of equal representation of the faculty body in comparison to the student population, she is also called upon by non BIPOC students and colleagues who are in need of a diverse panel or expertise specifically focused on media representations of and the lives of Black women from a Black Feminist framework. For example, she worked with a non BIPOC student AY 2021/2022 on her thesis committee. After turning this student away twice, and guiding her toward other faculty, the student explained that there were no other faculty in CAS who were appropriate for her to ask. The student expressed to Jennifer that the chair of her committee believed that there were certain questions that they felt only Jennifer could assist in answering.

Given this service tax, which other faculty can be called upon to fulfill these needs? When reevaluating criteria for tenure and promotion, reviewers and decision makers must understand the connections between service and scholarly expertise. In Jennifer's case, service is a reflection of the areas of research and scholarship she accomplished. Professional service often requires placing it in a singular, mutually-exclusive category that exploits faculty expertise based on their record of research and scholarship. Put simply, because of Jennifer's prior and current record of scholarship, her expertise is often solicited for consultation across campus and beyond. As reviewers for tenure and promotion, allies of Black women can identify ways that service requests based on expertise may count as scholarship, and given the service tax, more weight can be assigned to academic service when evaluating candidates for tenure and promotion.

Action Step Two: Revise How Student Evaluations Are Used in Tenure/Promotion Material

Students, like faculty and administrators, can be both racist and sexist. When they sit down at the end of the semester to fill out their course evaluations, they bring their sexism and racism with them. For this reason, professional associations such as the American Association of University Professors and the American Sociological Association (ASA) advise against using student teaching evaluations (STEs) in decision making for hiring and promotion, referring to them as "problematic" and "weakly related to other measures of teaching effectiveness and student learning" (ASA, 2019). Although some departments and universities have moved away from using STEs, this is not the norm.

Multiple studies confirm biases in the way BIPOC women, especially Black women, are evaluated by students (Bavishi et al., 2010; Basow et al., 2013; Chavez & Mitchell, 2020). Although the use of STEs disproportionately harms Black women, we all have a vested interest in using more reliable measures of teaching effectiveness and student learning. One of tenets of Black feminist theory states when the most marginalized are centered in activism, all other groups necessarily benefit (Neville & Hamer, 2001; DeFilippis & Anderson-Nathe, 2017). All instructors, regardless of their identity, should want to bar the use of STEs in hiring and promotion decisions.

Research shows everything from what time the course is taught to class size and subject matter can influence the results of our STEs (ASA, 2019). Other arbitrary characteristics such as age, "charisma", and whether or not the students perceive the instructor as physically attractive have also been found to influence students' perception of the course and the instructor (Boring & Ottobani, 2016). Issues regarding identity and course characteristics aside, many of us are scientists. Is it not problematic to draw conclusions from statistical data where response rates are ignored and distributions are unreported

(Boysen, 2015; Stark & Freishtat, 2014)? Surely, we can agree that STEs are not reliable enough data to be used when making life-changing decisions.

Many organizations do in fact advocate for holistic measures of teaching effectiveness such as peer-observation and self-evaluation. As noted in the AAUP "Statement on Teaching Evaluation,"

> Faculty members should be meaningfully involved in any systematic efforts to obtain student opinion. Cooperation among students, faculty, and administration is necessary to secure teaching performance data that can be relied upon. No one questionnaire or method is suitable to every department or institution... The important consideration is to obtain reliable data over a range of teaching assignments and over a period of time.
>
> Evaluations in which results go only to the individual professor may be of use in improving an individual teacher's performance, but they contribute little to the process of faculty review. Student input need not be limited by course evaluations. Exit interviews, questionnaires to alumni, and face-to-face discussion are other ways in which student feedback can be profitably gathered (2016).

Some propose making it optional to submit STEs, allowing the faculty under review to decide whether or not they want to provide their evaluations to hiring/promotion committees. While this is certainly a step in the right direction, hiring and promotion committees have come to expect STEs in portfolios. To ensure that Black women truly have the ability to withhold racist and sexist reviews of their teaching without penalty, we would need to somehow ensure that the absence of evidence *is not used as evidence*. Teresa Ciabaittari (ASA, 2019) suggests totally reframing the way we think of STEs—treating them as personal feedback as opposed to formal evaluation—so they are not even viewed as reliable indicators of teaching effectiveness. Removing them from the list of materials that can be submitted for promotion could ensure that if Black women decide not to submit their STEs, committee members cannot draw their own conclusions as to why they were withheld.

Action Step 3: Revise the Weight of Research and Scholarship for Tenure and

Promotion and Hold Those with Decision Making Authority Accountable!

Because of academia's racist and sexist history, Black women have only recently gained entrance to higher education at reputable numbers, both as faculty and students (Bell et al., 2020). As such, standards for tenure and promotion have largely been created without their input (Turner et al., 1999). Moreover, every department sets their own standards for which journals count as "scholarly" and what kinds of publications qualify as "suitable" for tenure and promotion. Bell et al. (2021) write, "We must all resist accepting the idea that journals formed by White men and published for most of their history with few to no editors, reviewers, and authors who were not White men, are better than those created in and built on more diverse foundations" (p. 48). As Olivia argues, fellow white women, in particular, have an obligation to fight for journals that emphasize intersectional and race-based research to be included in their department's list of "acceptable" journals.

Again, by centering Black women in this way white women also benefit. By that same token, in ignoring the disproportionate challenges facing Black women writers and researchers, white women hurt themselves. For example, Black women who write about Black feminism or race in scholarship often have fewer venues for submission where racial and/or Black studies are the primary foci or scope for the journal in comparison to mainstream or generalist disciplinary journals, many of which are often designated as "top-tier" or flagship journals. Thus, so long as Black women's scholarship, and the journals that are more receptive to their work, are viewed as "too subjective" to be valuable, the journals white women find homes in will similarly be denigrated by colleagues and within academia.

As previously acknowledged in Jennifer's tenure and promotion case, allies and decision makers must rethink the traditional weight that assigns to teaching, service and research/scholarship, especially because these categories are not mutually exclusive. In Jennifer's case, her service obligations and requests for consultation exist because of the expertise she possesses as an educator and scholar. Further, the traditional metrics institutions use to evaluate research and scholarship often disproportionately adversely affect Black women. For example, using H-indices and other metrics that measure the number of citations by Black feminists, do not account for the fact that our subjects may be controversial and not included in mainstream literature, and in particular, mainstream feminism. "The data is incontrovertible. Women of color are more likely to be denied tenure than others" (Torres, 2020, p. 158).

Additionally, such factors in evaluation of research and scholarship often fail to consider the intersecting and interdisciplinary fields where Black feminists disseminate their work. While feminist research methods allow for collaborative projects, white feminists often ignore race work that isn't exclusively grounded in feminism. For example, when Staci pursued promotion to full professor, the GWS faculty committee provided a negative recommendation because they only evaluated publications that were clearly noted as "feminist," and did not count any publications that mentioned race and other scholarly topics in her primary field of rhetoric and composition. Put simply, they cherry-picked and only counted the works that *they* could identify as feminist, even though the institution's collective bargaining agreement makes it clear that promotion achievements are in fact cumulative.

Finally, those who make tenure and promotion recommendations and decisions should be held accountable for their decisions. This includes department chairs, deans, and provosts. If there are reports of institutional biases that adversely affect such decisions, decision makers should be required to submit data and demographics of those who received tenure and promotion in contrast to those denied, and should report any disparities in academic rank across historically oppressed demographic groups. The report and recommendations must also explicitly state how the recommendation or decision takes into account any racial or gender disparities, including but not limited to service taxes that Black women typically pay in the academy.

Action Step 4: Equip Chief Diversity Officers and Institutional Equity Officers with Adequate Resources to Uphold both the Law and Restorative Justice

With the stories shared by Jennifer, Mariam, Staci and Keiondra, we found chief diversity and institutional equity offices inadequately resourced and insufficient to hold oppressors accountable. After Staci shared her story about her experiences in the Honors College with Black women administrators from other institutions, many remarked that we have to be careful dealing with those offices because they work on behalf of the university and not on behalf of its employees. Others simply said, those offices are never able to do anything because discrimination and retaliation are too hard to prove in a court of law. In other words, if nothing rises to a blatant or obvious violation of the law, in particular, Title IX or VII of the 1964 Civil Rights Act, nothing can be done. And despite the appearance of anti-bullying policies and workplace bullying modules aimed at preventing hostile work environments, many institutions continue to struggle in defining what constitutes bullying or harassment. Jennifer and Mariam found this to be true as well. In the case of both their 2020 complaints and 2022 complaints, they found that the OIE was either completely unresponsive or never formally opened an investigation; ultimately finding that they did not have enough evidence of harm.

But the data do not lie. When there's evidence of every BIPOC woman leaving a department or institution, or when BIPOC faculty are disproportionately not retained, there is a systemic problem. Therefore, how do we equip diversity and institutional equity offices as resources to train and support departments on microaggressions and bullying? What human resource practices can we adopt and apply that name these behaviors and provide the appropriate consequences for these behaviors? If institutional equity offices are relying on a true 51% preponderance of evidence standard—which states that retaliation, discrimination, or bullying more than likely occurred than did not occur—wouldn't this evidence correlate more strongly with the institutional data of faculty attrition? Simply put, institutions need to equip diversity and institutional equity offices with the authority and independence to identify and respond to complaints and prioritize justice more than protecting the institution from potential lawsuits.

Spaces for Healing/Recovery and Racial Reconciliation and Accountability

As Mariam, Jennifer, and Staci's narratives illustrate, there is still a need for reconciliation and accountability in order for real healing and recovery to occur. Perhaps the first step toward healing is an acknowledgment that Black women were harmed by the institution. While there has been some acknowledgment by a few select administrators at the institution, currently, there isn't an institutional acknowledgment that ensures accountability. As noted previously in this book, those inflicting harm still maintain their current ranks and roles at the institution, with the exception of Karen who was not granted a third term as GWS chair. Deans still have the authority to chastise Black women for the service tax and develop their own criteria and weights to what counts for tenure and promotion. In addition, while able to flee to a better and safer environment, Jennifer had to flee her primary disciplinary home of gender and women's studies, an outcome that potentially could have career-impacting effects on her research and professional trajectory.

Healing also requires systemic policy changes so that these behaviors don't recur. For instance, what systems might we put in place to prevent Black women from having to flee a toxic environment in the first place? What systems do we put in place that provide checks and balances in the ways that tenure and promotion decisions are made? What systems do we put in place to ensure that Black women in fact have due process when accused of misconduct? If these systems are in place within institutions and do exist on paper, how do we ensure that these processes are in fact followed?

Finally, true healing not only requires a change in systems, but also a change in outcomes. What good are policy changes if we do not increase the representation of Black women in faculty and leadership positions? What good are these policies if the demographics for academic rank remain the same? In the most recent climate survey at Mariam, Jennifer, and Staci's institution, many behaviors of bullying and claims of discrimination continue to go unchecked:

> Almost one in two employees at [our institution] (47%) have experiences [sic] or witnessed bullying. Over one-third of employee's report experiencing or witnessing discrimination, bias, and/or harassment based on gender (39%) and/or race/ethnicity (35%)... When asked to identify who initiated the offense over 50% of employees said faculty (54%), 50% said staff, 39% said students, 36% said other administrators, and 20% said senior administrator (vice president or dean)... Many employees (66%) did not report the incident(s). Top reasons the incidents were not submitted by employees included the employee not believing anything would happen (53%), a fear of retaliation (43%), feeling there was not enough evidence (33%), not believing [our institution] would support the employee (28%), not knowing who to report to (26%), fear of job loss (24%), decided it was not important enough (23%), or the employee had no witness for support (21%). For those who did report, the majority (64%) reported the incident(s) to their supervisor, followed by the Office of Institutional Equity (38%), a senior administrator (27%), Human Resources (27%), and a faculty member (19%) (McCorkle & Hesier, 2021, p. 16).

For healing to really happen, the data cannot resemble that as reflected above. Central to providing accountability is critically examining the role that leaders and administrators play in the incidents shared from the report. This data similarly mirrors the experiences that Mariam, Jennifer, and Staci previously shared; however, data in and of itself is not accountability. Illuminating and thus hopefully decreasing the adverse experiences of Black women within our institutions does provide evidence of accountability for healing to take place.

Concluding Remarks

As a collective, we have perhaps scratched the surface in relation to the actionable steps that universities can take to dismantle systemic racism, sexism, and misogynoir. What we have sought to do is begin the conversation about actionable steps: We purposefully offer a few examples of action, but have strategically chosen not to exhaust every possibility given the trauma we have all faced. In conclusion, we offer this: throw your feminism away, don't expect Black women to do your work.

To be more blunt, given the taxes, trauma, and intellectual labor we have already used and produced, we firmly believe that it is not always our responsibility to educate white people on how not to be racist and oppressive. We take great solace in beginning to heal from writing about these experiences, and we are greatly proud of the coup we've started. The stories within this book demonstrate that it is possible to create our own spaces and that we will not stay in places that are violent and oppressive. Calling upon Audre Lorde, silence had not served us in the past. Despite the potential risks in telling our stories, we are a collective who will continue to use our voices, not only in the service of our power, but also in serving the ideals of justice and equity for all in academia.

Our unified voices demand for the real work of the academy to begin. The bulk of that burden should not lie on Black women's labor. We have borne too many institutional costs to do the intellectual work of oppressors, allies, and accomplices. It is now your turn.

EPILOGUE OLIVIA'S "ACADEMIC KARENS" READING LIST

The following is a reading (and listening!) list for white feminists who are interested in being better feminists who are white. To be clear, these are materials I have found constructive. This is not an exhaustive or comprehensive list nor do I present the material in any particular order. Some deal explicitly with white feminism, some are pieces by Black feminists I love who sometimes speak to white women. In many ways this list is limited by my immersion in academic literature although there are some very accessible items on the list, including interactive pieces (e.g., Layla Saad's *White Supremacy and Me* workbook).

- *Everything You Already Know About Your Own Racism and How to do Better* (Regina Jackson and Saira Rao, 2022)
- "Kyla Schuller—The Trouble With White Women—With Brittany [sic] Cooper[1]," (*Politics and Prose* 2021), available on YouTube
- *Nice White Ladies* (Jessie Daniels 2021)
- "What's In a 'Karen'?", *Code Switch* (2020)
- "How to Not Be a Karen" ft. Mikki Kendall, *Unladylike* (2020)
- *White Supremacy and Me* (Layla Saad 2020)
- *Antagonizing White Feminism* (Chaddock and Hinderliter 2019)

- *They Were Her Property: White Women as Slave Owners in the American South* (Stephanie E. Jones-Rogers 2019)
- *Eloquent Rage: A Black Feminist Discovers Her Super Power* (Brittney Cooper 2018)
- "Unpacking White Feminism" lecture (Rachel Cargle 2018)
- "When Feminism Is White Supremacy in Heels" (Rachel Cargle 2018)
- *So You Want to Talk About Race* (Ijeoma Oluo 2018)
- *Unlikely Allies in the Academy: Women of Color and White Women in Conversation* (ed. Karen Dace 2012)

In signing off, may this reading list provide co-conspirators and white feminists with motivation so you will act, curiosity so you will listen, and humility so you remember to take a step back. May those triggered by these stories and analyses be healed, may those enraged stay enraged.

Notes

1 Note that Politics and Prose has misspelled Brittney Cooper's name. We use the misspelled version here as it appears in the title on YouTube.

REFERENCES

AAUP. (2016, April 13). *Statement on teaching evaluation*. Retrieved March 2, 2022, from https://www.aaup.org/report/statement-teaching-evaluation.

Adichie, C. *The Danger of a single story*. Talk presented at TEDGlobal 2009. Available at: www.ted.com/talks/chimamanda_adichie_the. *Sydney Law Review, 9*, 87–110.

Alexander, M. (2012). *The new Jim Crow: Mass incarceration in the age of colorblindness*. The New Press.

Alexander-Floyd, N. G. (2012). Disappearing acts: Reclaiming intersectionality in the social sciences in a post—black feminist era. *Feminist Formations, 24(1)*, 1–25.

American Sociological Association. (2019, September). *Statement on student evaluations of teaching*. Retrieved February 7, 2023, from https://www.asanet.org/wp-content/uploads/asa_statement_on_student_evaluations_of_teaching_feb132020.pdf

Ani, M. (2000). *Yurugu: An African-Centered critique of European cultural thought and behavior*. Trenton, NJ: Africa World Press.

Anthym, M., & Tuitt, F. (2019). When the levees break: The cost of vicarious trauma, microaggressions and emotional labor for Black administrators and faculty engaging in race work at traditionally White institutions. *International Journal of Qualitative Studies in Education, 32*(9), 1072–1093.

Anzaldúa, G. (1992). Mestiza consciousness. In C. R. McCann & S.-K. Kim (Eds.), *Feminist theory reader: Local and global perspectives* (pp. 277–284) Routledge.

Appiah, K. A. (2020). The case for capitalizing the B in Black. *The Atlantic*. https://www.theatlantic.com/ideas/archive/2020/06/time-to-capitalize-blackand-white/613159/

REFERENCES

Arnold, N., Osanloo, A. F., & Sherman Newcomb, W. (2021). Paying professional taxes for promotion and tenure: The costs of justice work for Black faculty. *Journal of Research on Leadership Education, 16*(2), 122–139.

Aziz, R. (1992). Feminism and the challenge of racism: Deviance or difference? In H. Crowley & S. Himmelweit (Eds.), *Knowing women: Feminism and knowledge* (pp. 291–305). Polity Press.

Baak, M., Miller, E., Sullivan, A., & Improving, K. H. (2005). Adichie, Chimamanda Ngozi. 'The Danger of a Single Story'. Talk presented at TEDGlobal 2009. Available at: www.ted.com/talks/chimamanda_adichie_the. *Sydney Law Review, 9*, 87–110.

Bailey, M. (2021). *Misogynoir transformed.* New York University Press.

Baker-Bell, A. (2020). *Linguistic justice: Black language, literacy, identity, and pedagogy.* Routledge.

Bambara, T. C. (1970). *The Black woman.* New York: Washington Square Press.

Banks-Wallace, J. (2002). Talk that talk: Storytelling and analysis rooted in African American oral tradition. *Qualitative Health Research, 12*(3), 410–426.

Barnett, B. M. et al. (1999). New directions in race, gender and class studies: African American experiences. *Race, Gender & Class, 6*(2), 7–28.

Barr, M. S. (2008). *Afro-future females: Black writers chart science fiction's newest new-wave trajectory.* The Ohio State University Press.

Basow, S., Codos, S., & Martin, J. (2013). The effects of professors' race and gender on student evaluations and performance. *College Student Journal, 47*(2), 352–363.

Bauder, D. (2021). *AP says it will capitalize Black but not White.* https://apnews.com/article/entertainment-cultures-race-and-ethnicity-us-news-ap-top-news-7e36c00c5af0436abc09e051261ffff1f

Bavishi, A., Madera, J. M., & Hebl, M. R. (2010). The effect of professor ethnicity and gender on student evaluations: Judged before met. *Journal of Diversity in Higher Education, 3*(4), 245.

Bell, M. P., Berry, D., Leopold, J., & Nkomo, S. (2021). Making Black Lives Matter in academia: A Black feminist call for collective action against anti-blackness in the academy. *Gender, Work & Organization, 28*, 39–57.

Betancourt, L., Yang, W., Brodsky, N., Gallagher, P., Malmud, E., Gianetta, J., Farah, M., & Hurt, H. (2011). Adolescents with and without gestational cocaine exposure: Longitudinal analysis of inhibitory control, memory and receptive language. *Neurotoxicol Teratol,* Jan–Feb: *33*(1), 36–46.

Bilge, S. (2013). Intersectionality undone: Saving intersectionality from feminist intersectionality studies. *Du Bois Review: Social Science Research on Race, 10*(2), 405–424.

Bloor, E. R. (1940). *We are many: An autobiography by Ella Reeve Bloor.* New York: International Publishers.

Bonilla-Silva, E. (2018). hilando fino. *Contexts, 17*(1), 26–27.

Boring, A., & Ottoboni, K. (2016). Student evaluations of teaching (mostly) do not measure teaching effectiveness. *Science Open Research, 0*(0), 1–11.

Boxer, M. J. (1998). Remapping the university: The promise of the women's studies Ph. D. *Feminist Studies, 24*(2), 387–402.

Boysen, G. A. (2015). Uses and misuses of student evaluations of teaching: The interpretation of differences in teaching evaluation means irrespective of statistical information. *Teaching of Psychology, 42*(2), 109–118.

Brewer, R. (1989). Black women and feminist sociology: The emerging perspective. *The American Sociologist, 20*(1), 57–70.

Browdy, R. (2018). Strong, Black, and woman: Examining self-definition and self-valuation as Black women's everyday rhetorical practices. *Reflections* Special Issue: Community resistance, Justice, and sustainability in the face of political adversity, pp. 7–36.

Brown, E. B. (1989). African–American women's quilting: Framework for conceptualizing and teaching African–American women's history. *Signs, 14*(4), 921–929.

Carby, H. V. (1996). White women listen! Black feminism and the boundaries of sisterhood. In H. A. Baker, M. Diawara, & R. H. Lindeborg (Eds.), *Black British cultural studies* (pp. 61–86). Taylor and Francis.

Carey, T. L. (2016). *Rhetorical healing: The reeducation of contemporary Black womanhood.* SUNY Press.

———. (2018). A tightrope of perfection: The rhetoric and risk of black women's intellectualism on display in television and social media. *Rhetoric Society Quarterly, 48*(2), 139–160.

Chadlock, N., & Hindliter, B. (2019). *Antagonizing white feminism: Intersectionality's critique of women's studies and the academy.* Rowman & Littlefield.

Chávez, K., & Mitchell, K. M. (2020). Exploring bias in student evaluations: Gender, race, and ethnicity. *PS: Political Science & Politics, 53*(2), 270–274.

Cho, S., Crenshaw, K. W., & McCall, L. M. (2013). Toward a field of intersectionality studies: Theory, application, and praxis. *Signs, 38*(4), 785–810.

Clinton, C. (1982). *The plantation mistress: Woman's world in the old south.* Pantheon Books.

Code, L. (1993). Taking subjectivity into account. In L. Alcoff & E. Potte (Eds.), *Feminist epistemologies* (pp. 83–100). Routledge.

Collins, P. H. (1986). Learning from the outsider within: The sociological significance of Black feminist thought. *Social Problems, 33*(6), s14–s32.

———. (1989). The social construction of Black feminist thought. *Signs: Journal of Women in Culture and Society, 14*(4), 745–773.

———. (1990). *Black feminist thought.* Unwin Hyman.

———. (1998). *Fighting words: Black women and the search for justice.* Minneapolis, MN: University of Minnesota Press.

———. (2015). Intersectionality's definitional dilemmas. *Annual Review of Sociology 41*, 1–20.

Cooper, B. C. (2015). Love no limit: Towards a Black feminist future (In theory). *The Black Scholar, 45*(4), 7–21.

———. (2017). *Beyond respectability: The intellectual thought of race women.* University of Illinois Press.

———. (2018). *Eloquent rage: A Black feminist discovers her superpower.* New York, NY: Picador.

Coursera. (2022). How long does it take to get a Phd? *Coursera*. Retrieved February 7, 2023, from https://www.coursera.org/articles/how-long-does-it-take-to-get-a-phd.

Cox, A. (2008). *Women of color faculty at the University of Michigan: Recruitment, retention, and campus climate.* Report Prepared for the University of Michigan Center for the Education of Women. Available online: http://www.cew.umich.edu/wp-content/uploads/2018/06/AimeeCoxWOCFull2_3.pdf.

Craig, C. L., & Perryman-Clark, S. M. (2011). Troubling the boundaries: (De) constructing WPA identities at the intersections of race and gender. *WPA: Writing Program Administration*, 34(2), 37–58.

Crenshaw, K. (1989). Demarginalizing the intersection of race and sex: A Black feminist critique of antidiscrimination doctrine, feminist theory and antiracist politics. u. *Chi. Legal f.*, 139.

Croom, N., & Patton, L. (2011). The miner's canary: A critical race perspective on the representation of Black women full professors. *Negro Educational Review*, 62/63(1–4), 13–39.

Daly, M. (1978). *Gyn/Ecology: The metaethics of radical feminism.*

Dankoski, M. (2000). What makes research feminist? *Journal of Feminist Family Therapy*, 12(1), 3–19.

Davis, A. Y. (1983). *Women, race, and class.* Village.

———. (2011). *Women, race, & class.* Vintage.

———, Dent, G., Meiners, E. R., & Richie, B. E. (2022). *Abolition. Feminism. Now* (Vol. 2). Haymarket Books.

DeBeauvior, S. (1952). *The second sex.*

DeFilippis, J. N., & Anderson-Nathe, B. (2017). Embodying margin to center: Intersectional activism among queer liberation organizations. In M. Brettschneider, S. Burgess & C. Keating (Eds.), *LGBTQ politics: a critical reader*, pp. 120—133. New York University Press.

Delaware, M. B. (2008). Planting seeds of change: Ela Baker's radial rhetoric. *Women's Studies in Communication*, 31(1), 1–28.

Dery, M. (1994). Black to the future: Interviews with Samuel R. Delany, Greg Tate, and Tricia Rose. In M. Dery (Ed.), *Flame wars* (pp. 179–222). Duke University Press.

Devault, M. L. (1999). *Liberating method: Feminism and social research.* Temple University Press.

DiAngelo, R. (2016). White fragility. *Counterpoints*, 497, 245–253.

———. (2018) *White fragility: Why it's so hard for white people to talk about racism.* Boston, MA: Beacon Press.

Dill, B. T. (1983). Race, class, and gender: Prospects for an all-inclusive sisterhood. *Feminist Studies*, 9(1), 131–150.

Donovan, J. (1996). *Feminist theory: The intellectual traditions of American feminism.* Continuum.

———. (2006). Feminism and the treatment of animals: From care to dialogue. *Signs: Journal of Women in Culture and Society*, 31(2), 305–329.

Durodoye, R., Gumpertz, M., Wilson, A., Griffith, E., & Ahmad, S. (2020). Tenure and promotion outcomes at four large land grant universities: Examining the role of gender, race, and academic discipline. *Research in Higher Education*, 61(5), 628–651.

Einstein, Z. (1981). *The radical future of liberal feminism.* Longman Publishing Group Longman.

Elshtain, J. B. (1981). *Public man, private woman.* Princeton University Press.

Ekpe, L., & Toutant, S. (2022). Moving beyond performative allyship: A conceptual framework for anti-racist co-conspirators. In K.F. Johnson, N.M. Sparkman-Key, A. Meca, & S.Z. Tarver (Eds.), Developing anti-racist practices in the helping professions: Inclusive theory, pedagogy, and application (pp. 67—91). Palgrave Macmillan.

Fabius, C. D. (2016). Toward an integration of narrative identity, generativity, and storytelling in African American elders. *Journal of Black Studies*, 47(5), 423–434.

Feagin, J., & Bennefield, Z. (2014). Systemic racism and US health care. *Social Science & Medicine*, 103, 7–14.

Firestone, S. (1970). *The eialectic of sex*. Bantam Books.

Flaherty, C. (2020, October 21). *The souls of black professors*. Inside Higher Ed. Retrieved February 7, 2023, from https://www.insidehighered.com/news/2020/10/21/scholars-talk-about-being-black-campus-2020.

Fonow, M. M., & Cook, J. A. (Eds.). (1991). *Beyond methodology: Feminist scholarship as lived research*. Indiana University Press.

———. (2005). Feminist methodology: New applications in the academy and public policy. *Signs* 30(4), 2211–2236.

Fox-Genovese, E. (1991). *Feminism without illusions*. University of North Carolina Press.

Frances Willard House Museum and Archives. Frances Willard House Museum & Archives. (2023, February 2). Retrieved February 7, 2023, from https://franceswillardhouse.org/.

Frankenberg, R. (1993). Growing up white: Feminism, racism and the social geography of childhood. *Feminist Review*, 45(1), 51–84.

Freedman, E. B. (1981). *Their sister's keepers: Women's prison reform in America 1830–1930*. University of Michigan Press.

Friedan, B. (1963/2010). *The feminine mystique*. Norton.

Garrett, S. D., and Turman, N. (2019). Finding fit as an "outsider within" a critical exploration of Black women navigating the workplace in higher education. In B. Reece, V. Tran, E. DeVore, & G. Porcaro (Eds.), *Debunking the myth of job fit in higher education and student affairs* (pp. 119–146). Stylus Publishing, LLC.

———, Williams, M. S., & Carr, A. M. (2022). Finding their way: Exploring the experiences of tenured Black women faculty. *Journal of Diversity in Higher Education*, 16(5), 527–538.

Gay, R. (2018). *Hunger: A memoir of (my) body*. New York: HarperCollins.

Gidings, P. (1984). *When and where I enter: The impact of Black women on race and sex in America*. Bantam.

Ginsberg, A. (2008). *The evolution of American women's studies: Reflections on triumphs, controversies, and change*. Springer.

Goerlick, S. (1991). Contradictions of feminist methodology. *Gender & Society*, 5(4), 549–477.

Gonzalez, P. (2021). *Retaining and supporting BIPOC professionals in PWIs: Addressing PWIs equity gap*. Doctoral dissertation, University of Southern California.

Griffin, K. A., Bennett, J. C., & Harris, J. (2013). Marginalizing merit?: Gender differences in Black faculty D/discourses on tenure, advancement, and professional success. *The Review of Higher Education*, 36(4), 489–512.

Guy-Sheftall, B. (1995). *Words of fire: An anthology of African–American feminist thought*. The New Press.

Guy-Sheftall, B., & Sanders, K. W. (1996). Educating black women students for the multicultural future. *Signs: Journal of Women in Culture and Society*, 22(1), 210–213.

Haley, S. (2016). *No mercy here: Gender, punishment, and the making of Jim Crow*. University of North Carolina-Chapel Hill Press.

Hamilton, T. K. (forthcoming). *Making a model system: The battle for educational equality in the nation's capital before Brown.* University of Chicago Press.

———. (2020). America's private, White, Elite Schools need reform. Now. *Momentum.* https://momentum.medium.com/the-death-of-diversity-a-call-for-radical-reform-in-pwis-3a5018065aa

Haraway, D. (1988). Situated knowledges: The science question in feminism and the privilege of partial perspective. *Feminist Studies, 14*(3), 575–599.

Harding, S. (1991). *Whose science? Whose knowledge?* Cornell University Press.

———. (2005). *The feminist standpoint reader.* Routledge.

Harriot, M. (2017, August, 29). The 5 types of 'Becky'. The Root. https://www.theroot.com/the-five-types-of-becky-1798543210.

Harris, A. P. (1997). Race and essentialism in feminist legal theory. In A. K. Wing (Ed.), *Critical race feminism: A reader* (pp. 11–18). New York University Press.

Harris-Perry, M. V. (2011). *Sister citizen: Shame, stereotypes, and black women in America.* New Haven, CT: Yale University Press.

Harstock, N. C. M. (1983). The feminist standpoint: Developing the ground for a specific feminist historical materialism. In S. Harding & Hintikka (Eds.), *Discovering reality: Feminist perspectives on epistemology, metaphysics, methodology, and the philosophy of science* (pp. 283–310). Reidel.

Haynes, C., Joseph, N. M., Patton, L. D., Stewart, S., & Allen, E. L. (2020). Toward an understanding of intersectionality methodology: A 30-year literature synthesis of Black women's experiences in higher education. *Review of Educational Research, 90*(6), 751–787.

Hekman, S. (1997). Truth and method: Feminist standpoint theory revised. *Signs: Journal of Women in Culture and Society, 22,* 341–365.

Hill, A. (2022). *Believing: Our thirty-year journey to end gender violence.* Penguin.

Hill, M. L. (2009). Wounded healing: Forming a storytelling community in hip-hop lit. *Teachers College Record, 111*(1), 248–293.

Hill Collins, P. (1986). Learning from the outsider within: The sociological significance of Black feminist thought. In M. Fonor & J. Cook (Eds.), *Beyond methodology: Feminist scholarship as lived research* (pp. 35–59). Indiana University Press.

———. (1991). *Black feminist thought.* Routledge.

———. 1996. What's in a name?: Womanism, black feminism, and beyond. *The Black Scholar, 24*(1), 9–17.

———. (1998). *Fighting words: Black women and the search for justice.* University of Minnesota Press.

hooks, b. (1981). *Ain't i a woman: Black women and feminism.* Boston, MA: South End Press.

———. (1994). *Teaching to transgress: Education as the practice of freedom.* New York: Routledge.

———. (2000a). *Feminist theory: From margin to center.* Cambridge, MA: South End Press.

———. (2000b). *Feminism is for everybody.* Boston: South End Press.

———. (2003). *Rock my soul: Black people and self-esteem.* New York: Atria Books.

———. (2005). *Sisters of the yam: Black women and self-recovery.* Boston: South End Press.

———. (2014). *Teaching to transgress.* Routledge.

REFERENCES

Hull, G. T., Bell-Scott, P., & Smith, B. (Eds.). (1982). *All the women are White, all the Blacks are men, but some of us are brave: Black women's studies*. Feminist Press.

Jackson, R., & Rao, S. (2022). *White women: Everything you already know about your own racism and how to do better*. Penguin Books.

Jaggar, A. (1983). *Feminist politics and human nature: Philosophy and society*. Rowman and Littlefield.

James, J., & Sharpley-Whiting, T. D. (2000). *The Black feminist reader*. Wiley.

Jayaratne T. E., Stewart A. J. (1991). Quantitative and qualitative methods in social sciences: Current feminist issues and practical strategies. In M.M. Fonow, & J.A. Cook (Eds.), *Beyond methodology: Feminist scholarship as lived research* (pp. 85–106). Bloomington, IN: Indiana University Press

Johnson, C. L. (1994). Participatory rhetoric and the teacher as racial/gendered subject. *College English*, 56(2), 409–419.

Jones, M. S. (2020). *Vanguard: How Black women broke barriers, won the vote, and insisted on equality for all*. Basic Books.

Jones-Rogers, S. E. (2019). *They were her property: White women as slave owners in the American South*. Yale University Press.

Jonsson, T. (2014). White feminist stories. *Feminist Media Studies* 14(6), 1012–1027.

Jordan, J. (1985). *Living room*. New York: Thunder's Mouth Press.

Jordan-Zachery, J. (2013). Now you see me, now you don't: my political fight against the invisibility/erasure of Black women in intersectionality research. *Politics, Groups, and Identities*, 1(1), 101–109.

Joseph, Gloria I. (1981). *Common differences: Conflicts in Black and White feminist perspectives*. Anchor Press/ Doubleday..

Joseph, G. I., & Lewis, J. (1986). *Common differences: Conflicts in Black and White feminist perspectives*. South End Press.

Kazmi, M. A., Spitzmueller, C., Yu, J., Madera, J. M., Tsao, A. S., Dawson, J. F., & Pavlidis, I. (2022). Search committee diversity and applicant pool representation of women and underrepresented minorities: A quasi-experimental field study. *Journal of Applied Psychology*,107(8), 1414–1427.

Kirsch, G. (1999). *Ethical dilemmas in feminist research: The politics of location, Interpretation, and publication*. State University of New York Press.

Larue, L. (1970). The Black movement and women's liberation. *The Black Scholar*, 1(7), 36–42.

Lawston, J. M. (2009). "We're all sisters": Bridging and legitimacy in the women's antiprison movement. *Gender & Society*, 23(5), 639–664.

Leary, J. D. (2005). *Post traumatic slave syndrome: America's legacy of enduring injury and healing*. Milwaukee, WI: Uptone Press.

LeFlouria, T. (2015). *Chained in silence: Black women and convict labor in the New South*. Chapel Hill: University of North Carolina Press.

Lerner, G. (1963). The Grimke sisters and the struggle against race prejudice. *The Journal of Negro History*, 48(4), 277–291.

Lester, B., Andreozzi, L., & Appiah, L. (2004). Substance use during pregnancy: Time for policy to catch up with research. *Harm Reduction Journal*, 1, Article number: 5.

Levine-Rasky, C. (2011). Intersectionality theory applied to whiteness and middle-classness. *Social Identities*, *17*(2), 239–253.

Lorde, A. (1976). *Between our selves*. Crested Butte, CO: Eidolon.

———. (1981). The uses of anger. *Women's Studies Quarterly*, *25*(1/2), 278–285.

———. (1983/2018). *The master's tools will never dismantle the master's house*. Penguin UK.

———. (1984). *Sister outsider*. Freedom, CA: The Crossing Press.

Lugones, M. (2003). *Pilgrimages/peregrinajes: Theorizing coalition against multiple oppressions*. Rowman & Littlefield Publishers.

Lynch, A. M., Barnett, K. B., & Green, M. T. (2022). Watching and waiting to exhale. In K. R. Hairston & T. G. Allen (Eds.), *The Ivory Tower: Perspectives of women of color in higher education* (pp. 7–26). Rowman & Littlefield.

Mann, S. A., & Patterson, A. S. (2016). *Reading feminist theory: From modernity to postmodernity*. Oxford University Press.

Maracle, L. (1996). *I am woman: A native perspective on sociology and feminism*. Press Gang Publications.

May, V. M. (2015). *Pursuing intersectionality, unsettling dominant imaginaries*. Routledge.

McCall, L. (2005). The complexity of intersectionality. *Signs*, *30*(3), 1771–1800.

Mccarthy, M. L. (2013). Sistership: Talking back to feminism. In *Ruptures: Anti-colonial & Anti-racist feminist theorizing* (pp. 51–57). Leiden, The Netherlands: Brill. Retrieved Mar 3, 2022.

McCorkel, J. A., & Myers, K. (2003). What difference does difference make? Position and privilege in the field. *Qualitative Sociology*, *26*(2), 199–231.

McCorkle, C., & Heiser, C. (2021). *Office of diversity and inclusion: 2020 Campus climate study report* (pp. 1–16).

McKenzie, M. (2015). *How can white women include women of color in feminism?' is a bad question. Here's why*.

McKissack, P. (1944–2017). (1992). *Sojourner Truth: Ain't I a woman?* Scholastic.

McLaughlin, O. M. (2020). *Politically and historically bound: Examining whiteness and intersectionality among self-identified feminists* (Unpublished doctoral dissertation). Western Michigan University, Kalamazoo, MI.

———. (forthcoming). *"I'm an intersectional feminist but…": White women's beliefs about race and women's oppression*. Manuscript in preparation.

Merriam-Webster. (2021). *An editor's guide to the Merriam-Webster January 2021 update*. https://www.merriam-webster.com/words-at-play/merriam-webster-style-and-usage-changes-january-2021#:~:text='Black'%20as%20an%20Adjective%20and,identified%20as%20being%20typically%20capitalized.

Mies, M. (1982). *The lace maker of Narspur: Indian housewives in the world market*. ZED.

Mohanty, C. (1988). Under Western eyes: Feminist scholarship and colonial discourses. *Feminist Review*, *30*, 61.

Mohanty, C. T. (1989). On race and voice: Challenges for liberal education in the 1990s. *Cultural Critique*, *14*, 179–208.

———. (2003). *Feminism without borders*. Duke University Press.

Naples, N. (2003). *Feminism and methodology*. Routledge.

Nelson, T., Brown, M. J., Garcia-Rodriguez, I., & Moreno, O. (2021). Gendered racism, anxiety, and depression: the mediating roles of gendered racialized stress and social isolation. *Ethnicity & Health*, 28(1), 1–17.

Nielson, J. M. (1990). *Feminist research methods: Exemplary readings in the social sciences*. Westview Press.

Neville, H. A., & Hamer, J. (2001). "We make freedom" an exploration of revolutionary Black feminism. *Journal of Black Studies*, 31(4), 437–461.

Newman, L. M., & Newman, L. M. (1999). *White women's rights: The racial origins of feminism in the United States*. Oxford University Press on Demand.

O'Conner, M. (2013). Special places in hell: A brief history of Taylor Swift's 'special place in hell for women'. *The Cut*, March 6, 2013. Retrieved October 13, 2017. https://www.thecut.com/2013/03/brief-history-of-taylor-swifts-hell-quote.html

Okun, T. (2021). White supremacy culture—still here. *Dismantlingracism.org* Retrieved September 24, 2021.

Olson, L. (2001). *Freedom's daughters: The unsung heroines of the civil rights movement from 1830 to 1970*. Simon and Schuster.

Ortega, M. (2006). Being lovingly, knowingly ignorant: White feminism and women of color. *Hypatia*, 21(3), 56–74.

Ortiz, A. T., & Briggs, L. (2003). The culture of poverty. Crack babies, and welfare. *Social Text*, 21(3), 39–57.

Painter, N. (1996). *Sojourner truth: A life, a symbol*. W.W. Norton.

Palmer, P. M. (1983). White women/Black women: The dualism of female identity and experience in the United States. *Feminist Studies*, 9(1), 151–170.

Perlow, O. N., Wheeler, D. I., Bethea, S. L., & Scott, B. M. (Eds.). (2018). *Black women's pedagogies: Resistance, transformation & healing within and beyond the higher education classroom*. Palgrave MacMillan: New York and London.

Perryman-Clark, S. M. (2016). Who we are (n't) assessing: Racializing language and writing assessment in writing program administration. *College English*, 79(2), 206–211.

Perryman-Clark, S. (2019). Race, teaching assistants, and workplace bullying. In C.L. Edler & B. Davilla (Eds.), *Defining, locating, and addressing bullying in the WPA workplace*. (pp. 124–127). Utah State University Press.

Perryman-Clark, S. M., Richardson, J., & Konate, M. (2022, March 1). A time to dream: Black women's exodus from White feminist spaces. *Present Tense*, 9(2). Retrieved March 3, 2022, from https://www.presenttensejournal.org/volume-9/a-time-to-dream-black-womens-exodus-from-white-feminist-spaces/

Potter, H. (2015). *Intersectionality and criminology: Disrupting and revolutionizing studies of crime*. Routledge.

Pough, G. D. (2004). *Check it while I wreck it: Black womanhood, hip-hop culture, and the public sphere*. Northeastern University Press.

Press, M. K. (1970). *Sexual politics*. University of Illinois Press.

Rafter, N. H. (1990). *Partial justice: Women, prisons, and social control*. Transaction Publishers.

Reger, J. (2014). The women's movement. In Hein-Anton van der Heijden (Ed), *Handbook of political citizenship and social movements* (pp. 418–439). Edward Elgar Publishing.

Reinharz, S. (1992). *Feminist methods in social research*. Oxford University Press.
Richardson, J. L. (2018). Healing circles as Black feminist pedagogical interventions. In O.N. Perlow, D.I. Wheeler, S.L. Bethea & B.B.M. Scott (Eds.), *Black women's pedagogies: Resistance, transformation & healing within and beyond the higher education classroom*. New York and London: Palgrave MacMillan.
Richardson-Stovall, J. (2012). Image slavery and mass media pollution: Popular media, beauty, and the lives of black women. *Berkeley Journal of Sociology: A Critical Review, 56*, 73–100.
Rideau, R. (2021). "We're just not acknowledged": An examination of the identity taxation of full-time non-tenure-track Women of Color faculty members. *Journal of Diversity in Higher Education, 14*(2), 161.
Rodriguez, S. S. (2015). *On becoming [Unfukwitable]*, Garden Theater, Detroit, MI. April 25, 2015.
Rosenthal, N., Fingrutd, M., Ethier, M., Karant, R., & McDonald, D. (1985). Social movements and network analysis: A case study of nineteenth-century women's reform in New York State. *American Journal of Sociology, 90*(5), 1022–1054.
Roth, B. (2004). *Separate roads to feminism: Black, Chicana, and White feminist movements in America's second wave*. Cambridge University Press.
Roth, J. (2017). Feminism otherwise: Intersectionality beyond occidentalism. *InterDisciplines. Journal of History and Sociology, 8*(2), 97–122.
Schwitzer, A. M., Griffin, O. T., Ancis, J. R., & Thomas, C. R. (1999). Social adjustment experiences of African American college students. *Journal of Counseling & Development, 77*(2), 189–197.
Sev'er, A., & Yurdakul, G. (2001). Culture of honor, culture and change. *Violence against Women, 7*(9), 964–998.
Smith, D. (1987). *The everyday world as problematic: A feminist sociology*. Northeastern University Press.
———. (1990). *The conceptual practices of power: A feminist sociology of knowledge*. Northeastern University Press.
Smith, V. (1989). Black feminist theory and the representation of the 'other'. *African American Literary Theory: A Reader*, 369–384.
Smith, J. L., Vidler, L. L., & Moses, M. S. (2022). The "Gift" of time: Documenting faculty decisions to stop the tenure clock during a pandemic. *Innov High Educ, 47*, 875–893. https://doi.org/10.1007/s10755-022-09603-y
Sprague, J., & Zimmerman, M. (1993). Overcoming dualisms: A feminist agenda for sociological methodology. In P. England (Ed.), *Theory on gender/gender on theory* (pp. 255–280). Aldine Press.
Stacey, J. (1988). Can there be a feminist ethnography? *Women's Studies International Forum, 11*(1), 21–27.
———, & Thorney, B. (1985). The missing feminist revolution in sociology. *Social Problems, 23*(4), 301–316.
Stack, C. (1970). *All our kin*. Harper & Row.
Stanley, L., & Wise, S. (2013). Method, methodology and epistemology in feminist research processes. In *Feminist praxis* (pp. 20–60). Routledge.

REFERENCES

Stanton, E. C., & Douglass, F. (2011). Declaration of sentiments (1848). In *Treacherous texts* (pp. 20–23). Rutgers University Press.

Stark, P., & Freishtat, R. (2014). An evaluation of course evaluations. *ScienceOpen*. Center for Teaching and Learning, University of California, Berkeley.

Stewart, M. (1831). Religion and the pure principles of morality, the sure foundation on which we must build. *Maria W. Stewart: America's First Black Woman Political Writer*, 27–42.

Stockman, F. (2017). Women's March on Washington opens contentious dialogues about race. *New York Times*. Accessed on December 21, 2022. https://www.nytimes.com/2017/01/09/us/womensmarch-on-washington-opens-contentious-dialogues-about-race.html

Tauke, B., Smith, K., & Davis, C. (Eds.). (2015). *Diversity and design: Understanding hidden consequences*. Routledge.

Taylor, U. (1998). The historical evolution of black feminist theory and praxis. *Journal of Black Cultural Studies*, 29(2), 234–253.

Taylor-Mill, H. (1970). Enfranchisement of women. In S. Rossi (Ed.), *Essays on sex equality* (pp. 89–122). University of Chicago Press.

Terborg-Penn, R. (1998). *African American women in the struggle for the vote, 1850–1920*. Indiana University Press.

Thatcher, S. M., Hymer, C., & Arwine, R. (2023). Pushing back against power: Using a multilevel power lens to understand intersectionality in the workplace. *Academy of Management Annals*, 17(2), 710–750.

The Combahee River Collective. (1977). A Black feminist statement. In Guy-Sheftall (Ed.), *Words of fire: An anthology of African–American feminist thought* (pp. 232–240). The New Press.

Thompson, B. (2002). Multiracial feminism: Recasting the chronology of second wave feminism. *Feminist Studies*, 28(2), 336–360.

Thornton, D. M. (1983). Race, class and tender: Prospects for an all-inclusive sisterhood. *Feminist Studies*, 9(1), 132–150.

Tipirneni, R. (2021). A data-informed approach to targeting social determinants of health as the root causes of COVID-19 disparities. *American Journal of Public Health*, 111(4), 620–622.

Tong, R. (1989). *Feminist thought: A more comprehensive introduction*. Westview Press.

Torres, L. (2020). The struggle continues: Women of color faculty and institutional barriers. In J. Shayne (Ed.), *Persistence is resistance: Celebrating 50 years of gender, women & sexuality studies*. University of Washington Libraries.

Turner, C. S. V., Myers Jr., S. L., & Creswell, J. W. (1999). Exploring underrepresentation: The case of faculty of color in the Midwest. *The Journal of Higher Education*, 70(1), 27–59.

Ulman, S. E. (2005). Interviewing clinicians and advocates who work with sexual assault survivors: A personal perspective on moving from quantitative to qualitative research methods. *Violence Against Women*, 11(9), 1130–1139.

Wagner, A., & Lynn Magnusson, J. (2005). Neglected realities: Exploring the impact of women's experiences of violence on learning in sites of higher education. *Gender and Education*, 17(4), 449–461.

Walkington, L. (2017). How far have we really come? Black women faculty and graduate students' experiences in higher education. *Humboldt Journal of Social Relations, 39,* 51–65.

Wallace, M. (1995). Anger in isolation: A Black feminist's search for sisterhood. In Beverly Guy-Sheftal (Ed.), *Words of fire: An anthology of African American feminist thought.* The New Press.

Wells-Barnett, I. (1900). Lynch law in America. *Arena, 23*(1), 15–24.

West, C. (2021, July 13). This is my candid letter of resignation to my Harvard Dean. I try to tell the unvarnished truth about the decadence in our market-driven universities! let us bear witness against this spiritual rot! pic.twitter.com/hclaunswdu. *Twitter.* Retrieved February 7, 2023, from https://twitter.com/CornelWest/status/1414765668222869508?ref_src=twsrc%5Etfw%7Ctwcamp%5Etweetembed%7Ctwterm%5E1414765668222869508%7Ctwgr%5E76dc4104f4d83570428da6fef644d478b80c53b1%7Ctwcon%5Es1_&ref_url=https%3A%2F%2Fwww.npr.org%2F2021%2F07%2F13%2F1015632217%2Fcornel-west-has-announced-hes-leaving-harvard-and-says-the-school-has-lost-its-w.

West, N. M. (2022). Embodying Black feminist epistemology to make green grass grow: The transition from administrator to academic for a Black woman in student affairs. *Journal of Diversity in Higher Education, 15*(5), 630–642.

Williams, A. (2020). Black memes matter: #LivingWhileBlack with Becky and Karen. *Social Media + Society, 6*(4). https://journals.sagepub.com/doi/10.1177/2056305120981047

Winchester III, W. W. (2019). Engaging the black ethos: Afrofuturism as a design lens for inclusive technological innovation. *Journal of Futures Studies, 24*(2), 55–62.

Wolf, D. L. (1996). *Feminist dilemmas in fieldwork.* Westview Press.

Yarbrough, M., & Bennett, C. (2000) Cassandra and the Sistahs: The peculiar treatment of African American women in the myth of women as liars. *Journal of Gender, Race and Justice, 3,* 625–657.

Yasek, L. (2006). Afrofuturism, science fiction, and the history of the future. *Socialism and Democracy, 20*(3). http://sdoline.org/42/afrofuturism science-fiction-and-the-history-of-the-future.

Yee, S. J. (1992). *Black women abolitionists: A study in activism, 1828–1860.* University of Tennessee Press.

INDEX

A

academic institutions, 55
Academic Labor Relations Contract Administrator, 64
accountability, 45, 49, 116. 117, 132–4
   administrative, 135–8
   and racial reconciliation, 144–6
   white folks, 132–4
activism, 4
administrative accountability, 135–8
administrative appointment, 83
African American and African Studies Program (AAAS), 52, 79, 80
Africana Studies (AFS) Program, 33, 34, 51, 52
   teacher- scholar, 33–5
afrofuturism, 90–6
Ain't I A Woman: Black Women and Feminism, 7, 27
Alexander- Floyd, Nikol, 28
allyship, 7

American Association of University Professors (AAUP) Union, 34, 36, 60, 68, 71
Annual Review process, 100–1
Antagonizing White Feminism, 104
anti-Blackness
   events, 41
   on harm and healing in academy, 8–12
anti-poverty/pro-socialist organizing, 121
anti-racism, 134
antisemitism, 106
anti-sexism, 134

B

Baker, Ella, 21
BIPOC women, 83
   in academic spaces, 87–8
   humiliation and consequences, 92
   investigations and backstabbing, 87–8
   as mammies, 84–5
   technical surveillance, 91

trauma and institutional abuse, 88–90
birth control movement, 121
Black Americana Studies Program, 50
Black Diasporic magic, 71
Black Feminist framework, 139
Black feminist methods, 104
Black feminist theory, 74
    in the Academy, 26–30
Black Feminist Thought (1990), 27
Black Liberation and Second Wave, 20–5
Black liberation movement, 22
Black male chauvinism, 23
Black women
    in academic spaces, 2
    conceptualizations of sisterhood, 118–23
Black Women: Shaping Feminist Theory, 27
Bloor, Ella Reeve, 127, 128

C

chief diversity officers, 143–4
civil rights, 21
Civil Rights Act of 1964, 22
Civil Rights movement, 21
cognitive dissonances, 9
College of Arts and Sciences (CAS)
    administration, 34, 35, 69, 139
Collins, Patricia Hill, 115, 116
Combahee River Collective, 25
compulsory sterilization, 121
coping and therapeutic mechanisms,
    learning resources, 73–4
counterproductive response, 107
Crandall, Prudence, 125–7
Crenshaw, Kimberlé, 29
critical analysis of power, 29
critical race theory (CRT), 79
critical whiteness studies and research,
    97, 108
crooked rooms, 1

D

Davis, Angela, 22
Declaration of Independence, 122
Declaration of Sentiments (1848), 120
"Demarginalizing the Intersection of Race
    and Sex" (1989), 28
departmental teaching assistantship, 99
Dill, Thornton, 129
discounting, 2–3
discrimination, 104

E

early Black feminism, 17–20
education leadership, 11
Eloquent Rage book club, 134
emphasis on praxis, 5
epistemological frameworks, 7
erasure in white feminist circles, 2–3
Eurocentric perspective, 8

F

Family and Medical Leave (FMLA),
    40, 85, 92
Family Educational Rights and Privacy Act
    (FERPA) guidelines, 63, 64, 69
Feminine Mystique, 23
Feminism in the Late 20th Century, 26–30
feminist activism, 4
    and spaces, 5
feminist genealogies, 3–8
    and art of storytelling, 13–31
Floyd, George, 41
funding sources, 98

G

gender and women's studies (GWS), 33–5,
    35, 36, 39

dismantling, 46
mental health concerns, 44
tenure legacy, 43
tolerated difference, 47
toxicity, 35–7
gender equality, 5
gender equity, 38
gender systems, 20
Graduate Student Association (GSA), 102, 110, 114
grounding artifacts, 76

H

Harris- Perry, Melissa, 1
"Healing Circles as Black Feminist Pedagogical Interventions," 73
healing/ recovery, 144–6
Honors College, 82
human-centered design (HCD) approaches, 93

I

Institute for Intercultural and Anthropological Studies (IIAS), 40, 48, 95
institutional accountability, 79
institutional cultures, 81–2
institutional equity officers, 143–4
institutional racism, 6
institutional vulnerability, 94
intellectual theorizing, 4
Intercultural and Anthropological Studies (IIAS), 95
International Labor Defense convention, 128
intersectional approaches to liberation, 107, 117
intersectional feminist analysis, 112, 124
intersectionality, 7, 109
 subject position of Black women, 7

K

Keiondra's story, 98–103

L

law and restorative justice, 143–4
learning resources of coping and therapeutic mechanisms, 73–4
Lorde, Audre, 2

M

marginalization, 2–3, 53
masculinity, 22
maternal cocaine use, 10
McKenzie, Mia, 9
mid-20th century black feminism, 20–25
Mohanty, Chandra, 28
monolithic body of knowledge, 4
mutual liberation, 125

N

National American Women's Suffrage Association (NAWSA), 3, 120
National Black Feminist Organization (NFBO), 24
National Woman Suffrage Association (NWSA), 120
National Women's Organization (NOW), 23, 24

O

Office of Institutional Equity (OIE), 38, 39, 47, 48, 59, 66
Olivia's Story, 103–108
oppression, 5
 forms of, 5

tactics, 70
oral traditions and silencing of Black women, 14–17

P

Painter, Nell, 130
parental rights, 10
politics and toxic culture, 37–8
population control of "underclasses," 121
praxis-based framework, 4, 11
pre-existing academic programs, 103
prenatal cocaine use, 9
professional activity report, 86
prospects for all-inclusive sisterhood, 118, 129
PTSD, 55–56, 80
public sociology, 104

R

race and ethnicity scholar, 110
race- traitor, 31
racial justice, 5
racial reconciliation, 144–6
racism, 2–3, 5
radical self- care and well- being, 73
resilience, 55
restorative justice, 49

S

Second Wave, 20–25
self-actualization, 65
self-care, 72
self-empowerment, 65
self-love, 72
service tax, 138
shared victimization, 122
sisterhood, 118–23
Sister Outsider: Essays and Speeches, 6, 25

social hierarchy, 5
social transformation, 73
sociology, 57
Southern Christian Leadership Conference (SCLC), 21
storytelling, 2–3
Student Nonviolent Coordinating Committee (SNCC), 21, 23

T

tenure and promotion review, 139–41
research and scholarship, 141–3
"third wave" feminism, 26
Third World Women's Alliance (TWWA), 22, 23
transgender therapies, 81
Tubman, Harriet, 25

V

vanguard center, 23
visceral reactions, 9
Voting Rights Act of 1965, 22

W

War on Poverty, 10
white feminist movements, 4
white feminist terrorism, 55–80
white feminist toxicity, 37–40
white folks, accountability, 132–4
White Supremacist and Feminist Spaces, 47–50
Willard, Frances, 121
Women's Christian Temperance Union, 121
Women's Liberation Movement, 121–2
women's liberation movement, 24
Women's March on Washington (WMW), 122–3
Women's Studies Program (WMS), 34, 35

AUTHOR BIOGRAPHIES

Dr. Jennifer L. Richardson is Associate Professor of African American and African Studies at Western Michigan University. As a Black feminist sociologist, her work focuses on intergenerational African Ring Shout healing circles as pedagogical and methodological approaches, Africana women's collective healing as a socio-political path to the recovery of self, and the ways Black women navigate the intersections of media, beauty, and identity.

Dr. Mariam Konaté is a Professor of African American and African Studies and of Gender and Women's Studies at Western Michigan University. Her research interests include the experiences of Continental African immigrants in the USA, the relevance of father absence to African American women's heterosexual dating experiences, skin bleaching, comparative literature and cultural studies, African epics, and Post-Colonial Studies.

Dr. Staci M. Perryman-Clark is Interim Dean of Merze Tate College and Professor of English and African American Studies at Western Michigan University. As an experienced administrator, she has led and developed key diversity, equity and inclusion initiatives and has received numerous honors from Western Michigan University, Conference on College Composition and Communication (CCCC) and Conference of Writing Program Administrators. Perryman-Clark is the 2023 chair of CCCC.

Dr. Olivia Marie McLaughlin is Assistant Professor of Sociology and Criminology at the University of Wisconsin-Whitewater. Her research focuses on the ways white women make sense of, and act on, their ideas about race, racism, and antiracism within feminism. She has published works on genocide studies, heuristics, and alternative pedagogies for undergraduate education.

Dr. Keiondra Grace is the Director of Research at Mothering Justice, a grassroots policy advocacy organization providing mothers of color with resources and tools to use their power to make equitable changes in policy. As a Black feminist scholar, she uses a blend of theory and practice to bolster services and supports aimed at alleviating inequalities and empowering people. Her research aims to generate knowledge that advocates for social action and policy reform on behalf of those historically placed at the margins.

EQUITY IN HIGHER EDUCATION
THEORY, POLICY, & PRAXIS

A BOOK SERIES FOR EQUITY SCHOLARS & ACTIVISTS

Dr. Elizabeth Powers, *General Editor*

Globalization increasingly challenges higher education researchers, administrators, faculty members, and graduate students to address urgent and complex issues of equitable policy design and implementation. This book series provides an inclusive platform for discourse about—though not limited to—diversity, social justice, administrative accountability, faculty accreditation, student recruitment, admissions, curriculum, pedagogy, online teaching and learning, completion rates, program evaluation, cross-cultural relationship-building, and community leadership at all levels of society. Ten broad themes lay the foundation for this series but potential editors and authors are invited to develop proposals that will broaden and deepen its power to transform higher education:

(1) Theoretical books that examine higher education policy implementation,
(2) Activist books that explore equity, diversity, and indigenous initiatives,
(3) Community-focused books that explore partnerships in higher education,
(4) Technological books that examine online programs in higher education,
(5) Financial books that focus on the economic challenges of higher education,
(6) Comparative books that contrast national perspectives on a common theme,
(7) Sector-specific books that examine higher education in the professions,
(8) Educator books that explore higher education curriculum and pedagogy,
(9) Implementation books for front line higher education administrators, and
(10) Historical books that trace changes in higher education theory, policy, and praxis.

Expressions of interest for authored or edited books will be considered on a first come basis. A Book Proposal Guideline is available on request. For individual or group inquiries please contact:

editorial@peterlang.com.

To order other books in this series, please contact our Customer Service Department at:

peterlang@presswarehouse.com (within the U.S.)
orders@peterlang.com (outside the U.S.)

Or browse online by series at www.peterlang.com